Southern Living GARDEN GUIDE
Shrubs

Series Editor: Lois Trigg Chaplin

Text by Glenn Morris

Oxmoor House®

Contents

Library of Congress Catalog Number: 95-74605
ISBN: 0-8487-2243-4
Manufactured in the United States of America
First Printing 1996

Editor-in-Chief: Nancy Fitzpatrick Wyatt
Editorial Director, Special Interest Publications:
Ann H. Harvey
Senior Editor, Editorial Services: Olivia Kindig Wells
Art Director: James Boone

Southern Living Garden Guide SHRUBS

Series Editor: Lois Trigg Chaplin
Assistant Editor: Kelly Hooper Troiano
Copy Editor: Jennifer K. Mathews
Editorial Assistant: Laura A. Fredericks
Garden Editor, *Southern Living*: Linda C. Askey
Indexer: Katharine R. Wiencke
Concept Designer: Eleanor Cameron
Designer: Carol Loria
Senior Photographer, *Southern Living*: Van Chaplin
Production and Distribution Director: Phillip Lee
Associate Production and Distribution Manager:
John Charles Gardner
Associate Production Managers: Theresa L. Beste,
Vanessa D. Cobbs
Production Coordinator: Marianne Jordan Wilson
Production Assistant: Valerie L. Heard

Our appreciation to the staff of *Southern Living*
magazine for their contributions to this book.

Pyracantha

Oakleaf hydrangea

Cover: *Southern Indian hybrid azalea*
Frontispiece: *Ligustrum*

Azalea

Shrubs Primer

A well-designed garden feels like another room of the house. Shrubs help create that room by providing a framework and adding to the decor.

Whether you are an experienced gardener seeking new greenery to polish an existing landscape or a beginner in search of solutions to common landscape problems, you need only look into the world of shrubs to find a plant that will suit your needs. Shrubs fit into the garden design between the "ceiling" of trees and the "floor" of grass and ground covers. They are a diverse group of plants that provide framework, color, texture, and fragrance to enhance your garden; strategically planted, they will make your garden functional as well.

First, you may ask, what are shrubs? In simple terms, shrubs are woody plants that branch at the base near ground level and typically do not have a central trunk like a tree. They may be ***evergreen,*** keeping their leaves year-round, or ***deciduous,*** shedding their foliage annually. Many shrubs are known for their blooms while others find favor for their strikingly sculptural form.

You will see shrubs that hug the ground and those that soar to 20 feet, becoming treelike in stature. Burford holly, for example, will easily reach a second-story window while Gumpo azalea is only knee-high. Most shrubs fall between these extremes; shrubs put on a show at or near eye level.

With a little planning and proper care, shrubs are an attractive and functional addition to your garden. This book will help you select the right shrub for your landscape and will see you through planting and caring for the shrub in years to come.

One essential component to any successful garden is the artful and creative use of shrubs.

Practical Benefits of Shrubs

Pink azaleas thrive under the high canopy of shade trees.

Shrubs can serve a practical role in the overall garden design. When planning your garden, remember their practical uses in addition to their decorative value.

Shrubs help create an outdoor room for you to enjoy, regardless of the size of your property. There are many ways to put shrubs to work in addition to relying on their ornamental qualities. A row of tall shrubs along a property line provides privacy and serves as a windbreak. Shrubs can also protect your property by preventing erosion by wind or water. You can plant shrubs to screen undesirable views at eye level; they screen more quickly and take up less space than trees. You may also incorporate shrubs for traffic control, planting them to redirect foot traffic across your property.

Filling In Under Trees

You can plant shrubs as a ground cover beneath trees where lawn grasses may struggle. This will eliminate the aggravation of a thin lawn in too much shade and will add greater interest to the garden during the year.

The key to such a planting is selecting shrubs that can adapt to the lower light beneath established trees and still be vigorous enough to compete with the trees for nutrients from the soil. Fortunately, there are many choices; camellias, rhododendrons, azaleas, andromeda, mahonia, and other shrubs thrive in such conditions if you water and fertilize them regularly during the first two years, until they become well established.

To visualize such a bed, use a garden hose to outline the shape in your garden, including all areas where lawn grasses struggle. When the bed is decided, kill any grass or weeds within the area with a nonselective herbicide, such as glyphosate. Establish a clean edge by using a shovel to dig a trench, or lay an edging of brick or other material around the bed. This makes it easier to mow around the bed and maintain the mulch within it.

Shrubs may be used to show off garden statues.

Do not till under the existing trees before planting as this may damage their root systems. However, you may bring in up to two inches of friable topsoil to cover the entire area without damaging the trees' feeder roots, provided you do not compact the soil with heavy equipment. This additional soil will assist in good, quick shrub growth. Plant the shrubs individually and avoid cutting large tree roots as you plant.

Creating Spaces

Using shrubs to define space in the garden is fundamental to garden design, though this functional use is often unintentional. For example, when you plant an evergreen screen, a privacy hedge, or a shrub border, you also install a wall of green. Shrubs that signal an entry or direct a visitor's eye along the sidewalk will give the lawn a different shape. Planting large shrubs along a sidewalk that parallels the front of the house will separate the entry from the greater expanse of lawn beyond the walk. Rhododendrons, camellias, aucubas, and other shade-loving shrubs may be arranged to create pockets beneath canopy trees. This gives depth to wooded areas of the garden. Such positioning of shrubs creates an outdoor room.

Low-growing shrubs, such as Helleri holly or Rotunda holly, physically separate you from one side of a garden but allow you to see across the barrier.

Hedges of dwarf English boxwood outline the beds of this formal parterre garden.

While such informal uses of shrubs are common, shrubs may also be trimmed into architectural hedges to establish pattern and geometry in a formal garden. English boxwood and some selections of Japanese holly make terrific sheared hedges for parterre herb gardens. Common boxwood or English boxwood may be used to line walks around the perimeter of a floral planting and may be trimmed into elegant low walls to contain the flowers.

Providing Privacy

Planting a hedge of shrubs can save you the expense of building a fence or a wall to provide privacy between your property and that of your neighbors. Shrubs are available in a variety of shapes and sizes and are less expensive than most building materials.

Privacy plantings do not need to be planted in a straight line, nor do they have to be a single species. A mixed border of evergreen shrubs will shield your property and add more garden interest. For example, you can combine Burford holly, camellia, and wax myrtle into one planting. Each shrub offers different seasonal effects for a very handsome living wall.

Large, fast-growing evergreens, such as ligustrum or wax myrtle, rapidly grow into a dense thicket. Because these plants will quickly grow to 8 feet wide and then continue expanding upward and outward, only a few well-placed plants are necessary. In shady locations, evergreen azaleas or rhododendrons may fill in between your property and that of your neighbors.

The immediate effectiveness of such a living fence is determined by the size of the plants you install. Using average-sized, fast-growing evergreen plants, you can expect an effective barrier within three to five years.

Screening

While a planting of shrubs may serve as a privacy planting that does not allow others to see in, it may also block the view from your property.

These treelike Burford hollies create a "gate" to this outdoor sitting area.

COMMON EVERGREENS FOR SCREENING		
Shrub	Recommended Spacing	Height after Five Years
Cleyera	3 feet	5 to 6 feet
Dwarf Burford holly	5 feet	5 to 6 feet
Fruitland elaeagnus	6 to 8 feet	8 to 10 feet
Ligustrum	4 to 8 feet	10 to 15 feet
Wax myrtle	6 to 8 feet	10 to 15 feet

A mixed screen of ligustrum and azaleas provide privacy and screen unwanted views.

To screen an unwanted view, you do not have to plant along the entire property line; instead, block only the offending view from the part of your property that you use most. Shrubs, especially evergreens, can target a specific item—a neighbor's woodpile or trash cans, for example—in a small planting.

You can weave a screen planting into the fabric of your garden by using it as the backdrop for a flower bed. Flowers naturally attract attention, so viewers will look at them and not look beyond the backdrop that is dutifully screening an unsightly view. Rapid-growing, dense evergreens, such as fruitland elaeagnus, ligustrum, and wax myrtle, are staples of this type of landscaping.

Do not discount vigorous deciduous shrubs, such as forsythia, weigela, peegee hydrangea, and the larger spireas. The branch network of these shrubs is so thick that they can be an effective screen even in winter.

If the view you want to shield is one from a second-story window, be certain that the shrub you choose will grow tall enough to do the job. Choose a shrub that has nearly treelike proportions and reaches at least 15 feet tall, such as Burford holly or wax myrtle.

Directing Traffic

Shrubs may also be used to encourage visitors to walk through your garden or around your lawn in a clear path. Use a shrub planting to clearly define the path; shrub beds send a logical signal: "walk here." Directional plantings also help your visitors decide the best areas through which to walk.

You can help provide security under windows with strategic plantings of wintergreen barberry, a tough, thorny evergreen shrub.

Deciduous shrubs, such as peegee hydrangea, direct traffic to the entry and separate it from the street.

A thick border of fruitland elaeagnus or Burford holly is as effective as a wall for prohibiting access.

Low plantings of Rotunda holly, yaupon holly, or rockspray cotoneaster can keep passersby from taking shortcuts across a lawn. Similar plantings work well around the edge of a terrace or a landing where the plants will spread to create a border.

Preventing Erosion

Shrubs can help stabilize the soil to prevent erosion. They create an umbrella with their foliage and help hold the soil in place with their vigorous root networks. A good root system is especially important in locations where water collects uphill and then washes over the sloped surface.

You can use shrubs to prevent erosion on steeply sloping areas of a lot where it may be dangerous to mow lawn grasses. Vigorous fibrous-rooted, low-spreading shrubs, such as rockspray cotoneaster, bearberry cotoneaster, and spirea, work very well. Large, mounding shrubs, such as forsythia and weigela, offer a different approach to the same problem. Once these are established, they cover a slope with a tangle of branches that will break up hard rainfall. They also establish a thick mat of roots that will help keep the soil in place.

Windbreaks

Coastal residents know the value of a windbreak: it keeps the wind from plying free the loose sand and carrying it away, as well as reducing the damage of salt spray on plants. Wax myrtle and ligustrum are indispensable as windbreaks in locations subject to salt spray, as are pittosporum and Indian hawthorn.

Windbreaks can also serve a valuable purpose inland, particularly in Zones 6 and 7, by deflecting cold winter winds. Fruitland elaeagnus and wintergreen barberry are two champion shrubs for this purpose. In shady locations, rhododendron and mountain laurel, both tough native plants, can be effective as well. From Zone 7 southward, look to ligustrum to shelter tender plants from winter's desiccation.

Low-growing Gumpo azaleas and Helleri hollies not only control foot traffic but also frame an open lawn.

Azaleas can perform such practical tasks as preventing erosion on sloping ground.

Aesthetic Benefits of Shrubs

The power of texture and form is evident in this evergreen seashore planting.

The closer you look at shrubs, the more you will see. Mix and match their leaf shapes, foliage colors, flowers, and fruit to enhance your garden.

The appeal of a shrub lies in its attributes. Its value may be the size of the leaves, the color of the foliage, the flower shape and color, or the fruit that follows the blooms. Blending textures, colors, flowers, and fruits is the beauty of creating a garden. Here is a look at some of the aesthetic qualities that shrubs may bring to your overall garden design.

Foliage

The leaves of a shrub are generally its strongest identifying feature. Whether a plant is evergreen or deciduous, the foliage is the most constant decorative trait that gives it appeal and lends the shrub to specific uses in the garden.

Texture and Size

A shrub's texture is a result of the size and the shape of the leaves. Unlike the form of a shrub, which you may alter by pruning and shearing, texture is constant. You will see that every shrub falls into one of three descriptive groups: fine textured, medium textured, and coarse textured.

• **Fine textured.** Shrubs with leaves typically less than 1 inch in length and breadth are classified in this group. Nandina, yaupon holly, spirea, and the boxwoods are examples. Fine-textured shrubs are more visually appealing when viewed at close range.

• **Medium textured.** This group includes shrubs with simple leaves (that have no lobes or indentations) measuring between 1 and 4 inches in length and rarely more than 1½ inches in width. Many species and selections are included in this group. Medium-textured shrubs blend together visually to become the backdrop planting against which fine- or coarse-textured shrubs generally serve as accents. Andromeda, cleyera, sasanqua camellia, mountain laurel, forsythia, most hollies, and azaleas are familiar shrubs of this classification.

• **Coarse textured.** This label is generally reserved for shrubs with leaves that are 4 inches long and 2 inches wide or larger, such as aucuba and rhododendron. Shrubs with ornate foliage, such as leatherleaf mahonia, an unruly growth habit, such as fruitland elaeagnus, or deeply lobed leaves, such as oakleaf hydrangea, also fall under this descriptive umbrella.

Because the foliage is outstanding in shape or size, coarse-textured plants will catch your eye from across the garden. This is also a key to their usage. Plant these shrubs to call attention to a particular location, such as a garden gate, a rock feature, or statues. You can also use them to interrupt the visual monotony of a sweep of undistinguished plantings. Rhododendron interplanted with mountain laurel and azaleas creates a composition with texture that is visually interesting when the shrubs are not in bloom.

Here is a handy rule of thumb for using texture: the shorter the distance from the shrub to the viewer, the easier it is to see the texture of the shrub. Thus, it is best to emphasize fine-textured shrubs in intimate settings where the plants will be seen up close, such as

The fine texture of common boxwood makes a good foil for perennials, such as hostas.

The coarse texture of rhododendron is always eye-catching.

A play of textures and foliage colors makes this garden corner lively. The light green, fine-textured new growth of nandina contrasts with the dark foliage of camellia.

courtyard gardens or adjacent outdoor sitting areas. Place coarse-textured shrubs farther from the viewer, such as across the garden from a sitting area. Unless planted specifically for contrast with fine-textured shrubs, coarse-textured shrubs can look out of scale and may overwhelm an intimate setting. However, a single mahonia or other coarse-textured shrub will serve as a fine accent in a small space when contrasted with a fine-textured shrub, a wall, or a fence.

The Foliage Color Palette

The color that you generally associate with a plant is the color of its leaves during the growing season. By choosing shrubs with a variety of foliage colors, you may add additional color interest that will be effective throughout the year. Foliage color will endow richness to your garden composition.

• **Green.** The more shrubs you consider, the more shades of green you will see. The range of greens spans from the deep, shiny green of Burford holly and Rotunda holly to the nearly chartreuse hues of Gold Flame spirea to the bluish cast of leatherleaf mahonia. In the garden, lighter green foliage seems casual and cheery while darker foliage has a more formal air and may be used to reinforce a design.

If you are using shrubs with approximately the same form, texture, and size, choosing plants with different foliage colors can distinguish the planting. For example, plant shrubs with lighter green foliage, such as oakleaf hydrangea, to bring a wooded setting out of the shadows. In contrast, depend on shrubs with darker foliage hues, such as camellia or Burford holly, to form a backdrop.

• **Variegation.** Some shrubs owe their primary ornamental qualities to a lack of green color along the margin of the leaf or places where the leaf is erratically patched with cream, red, or yellow. This coloring, in an otherwise green plant, is known as *variegation.* Aucuba, a coarse-textured, broad-leafed evergreen that prefers shade, is perhaps

The chartreuse foliage of Limemound spirea stands out against a dark background.

more widely known for its variegated selections, such as Mr. Goldstrike, than for the very handsome deep green species.

Because variegation is the exception, there is an element of surprise to plants with this coloring. As they are quite eye-catching, plant them where you want to draw attention. Use a variegated aucuba, for example, in a shady corner of the garden where you have placed a statue or a garden bench.

• **Other Colors.** While many shrub selections have variegated foliage, there are others with foliage that is tinted red, purple, or bronze, such as the dwarf Firepower nandina. Some even have maroon or bronze leaves, such as Crimson Pygmy barberry.

Use these unusually colored plants as accents; expect them to stand out vividly. The color of Crimson Pygmy barberry makes it one of the most useful shrubs for separating clashing foliage or flower colors. Plant it to bring a depth of color to a shrub border while keeping less harmonious plants apart.

• **Seasonal Colors.** The quality of a shrub's foliage color often changes with the season. In spring, when new growth emerges on evergreens, the seasonal change is spectacular. The soft, light green foliage paints the shrub with a fresh, youthful glow. The new growth of some shrubs, such as that of Mountain Fire andromeda, emerges a brilliant red in early spring. This unusual splash of color gives such shrubs more visual impact.

Deciduous shrubs can make a lovely, even spectacular fall color change, just as deciduous trees do. Among the best and brightest of the fall show are burning bush, which becomes a brilliant red, oakleaf hydrangea, which becomes russet, and baby's breath spirea, which glows with a golden hue.

After fall, shrubs such as cleyera and nandina take on a bronze to purple cast as their evergreen leaves are exposed to cold. This natural seasonal change brings additional interest at a time when evergreens are carrying the garden.

Blooms

All shrubs have a certain appeal throughout the year, but the flowering shrubs will dominate when they are in bloom. However, you should remember that this seasonal expression is also the shortest

Variegated aucuba brightens a shady corner.

The large white flowers of a single azalea lighten this intimate garden space.

period of show in the year-round life of a landscape plant, often lasting only two to four weeks.

Select several different flowering shrubs for each season to increase the variety in your garden and the effectiveness of blooms spread through the garden year. Always choose a few shrubs for their fragrance, too. Elaeagnus blooms are barely visible, but you can smell their sweetness from yards away.

The Floral Color Palette

Using color in the garden, whether foliage or flower, requires coordination of color schemes. Color in the garden captures the attention of the viewer. Well-blended color schemes or subtle dashes of bright hues that are well presented can give a garden zest and panache. Here are some color usage hints to help you get started.

• Be aware of the existing colors in your garden background. Do not use red or pink azaleas in front of a red brick structure; choose blooms that will coordinate.
• Avoid the use of shrubs that bloom simultaneously in conflicting colors, such as pinks and oranges.
• Concentrate color for emphasis. Let shrub color emphasize one portion or location in the garden at a time.
• Repeat a single color of blooms in several locations in the garden. Multiple uses of the same color create a sense of unity.
• Be bold with color contrast. The more vivid the contrast between an accent color and the backdrop, the more effective the accent will be.
• When viewed from a distance, masses of a single color are more effective than plantings of several colors.
• Bright colors, such as hot pink, appear to advance toward you and shorten the perception of distance while soft pastels or deeper colors recede, creating the illusion of greater space.
• Yellow in the garden is very buoyant and cheerful. Use it to lighten dark corners.

• Bronze or maroon is a great blending color. Use foliage or flowers of these shades to intercede between clashing colors.

• The eye tends to seek lighter colors, particularly in shady or dark settings. Remember this when you want to draw attention to (or from) a particular area.

• Variegated shrubs in masses may be overwhelming, especially if the variegation is bright and extensive. Use variegated plants sparingly for accents or to brighten small, dark areas.

Seasonal Blooms

Choose shrubs that bloom at different times during the year, not just in spring. While the exact time of bloom will vary according to your location, you can count on shrubs to bloom in a predictable sequence.

The order of bloom does not vary dramatically from north to south, but the calendar dates will be different between higher and lower latitudes. It is common for bloom times to vary four to eight weeks between warm and cold climates. For example, in the lower South, the flower season begins as early as January with shrubs like flowering quince, usually one of the earliest blooming shrubs, and leatherleaf mahonia, which rivals it for eagerness to bloom. March typically brings forsythia, native azaleas, and some hybrid azaleas in the deep South while April holds the greatest azalea show. In the upper South and farther north, quince may not bloom until March or April. Look for May as the month of rhododendron and mountain laurel; Gumpo azaleas bloom in May and June. June and July bring out the hydrangeas. One last native azalea, the plumleaf azalea, opens its scarlet trumpets in summer's heat and sometimes spills over into early August. In October, sasanqua camellia opens the camellia season, which can last into November and sometimes December.

If you plant shrubs with different blooming times, combine them in such a way that the peak of interest moves around the garden. Highlight one garden corner with early native azaleas (early spring) underplanted with Gumpo azaleas (early summer), and plant another corner with later-blooming sasanqua camellias (fall) and leatherleaf mahonia (late winter).

Ornamental Fruit

Many shrubs have ornamental berries or other fruit that follow the show of flowers at a time when there is little flower color in the landscape. For example, cranberry viburnum flares with fall color and

Pick a shrub that blooms in the "off season," such as camellia, for color in fall and winter.

The smooth architectural character of this residence is enlivened by the erratically branching, berry-covered pyracantha.

then begins the leafless months clad with abundant fruit. Cotoneasters sparkle back to life as their fruit ripens through fall; the berries are bright and showy in winter. The same is true of wax myrtle, which picks up a classy look with the addition of bright blue fruits on the female plants.

Nandina has profuse red berries that make it an even more indispensable shrub by rounding out a year of sustained ornamental interest. The bright berries of Burford holly are well-known mainstays of the winter landscape; their bright orange-red spots of color lighten the garden and hold the promise of visiting birds, such as cedar waxwings, swooping into the plantings to eat the fruit.

Although most shrubs present their berry show in fall and winter, the display of brightly colored fruit can begin earlier, such as the grape blue fruit of leatherleaf mahonia.

A few shrubs are worth having for the fruit alone. Plant beautyberry along paths or wooded driveways; you are not likely to notice it until fall, when it is covered with purple fruit. The fruit of pyracantha is so spectacular that this ornamental quality alone is the shrub's hallmark. Espalier pyracantha to a brick wall or a wooden structure, or plant it as a free-standing specimen where you may watch birds pick the plant clean of berries.

Selecting Shrubs

If you must have a garden problem, choosing from the wonderful array of shrubs is one of the most enjoyable difficulties to have. But where do you start? You may need shrubs to screen views, create spaces, or provide privacy. You might be concerned with the flowers, fragrance, form, and texture they will offer in your garden. Selecting shrubs can be a dilemma involving many choices, but if you first determine your needs, you can find the right shrub regardless of the growing conditions.

Size

While there is some variation in the ultimate size of a shrub due to local horticultural conditions, when you are told that a shrub will grow 8 feet tall, this usually means a minimum of 8 feet tall. The same is true of its width. Underestimating the growth rate and mature size of shrubs causes more landscape headaches than nearly any other oversight. That is why it is crucial to know the ultimate size—both height and width—that a shrub will reach. A plant that is knee-high when you bring it home may grow tall enough to reach the roof of your home and could be equally wide.

To select a shrub that properly fits a space, you must know your space limitations. Consider the height of eaves, overhangs, and power lines, as well as the width allowed by walls or walkways. In other words, do not put a shrub that may grow to 10 feet in a 4-foot space. If you find yourself constantly pruning a shrub because it is in the way, the shrub is in the wrong place. You should not have to fight a shrub; instead, select one that can grow to its normal size without crowding the location.

Size also affects how far apart you space shrubs at planting, and this spacing will affect your gardening budget. Unless a plant grows very slowly, it is better to space plants far enough apart to allow them to grow to their ultimate size. If you are planting shrubs that will eventually spread to 5 feet, plant them at least 4½ feet apart. In the long run, this is better for the plants and for your budget.

Because shrubs make up a huge group of plants, it helps to categorize them by size, as their size is generally the first and most important reason for choosing (or rejecting) a particular shrub for the landscape. You can classify them as low, medium, or tall. Even if you do not always know the particular plant you want, you will know the size that it must be in order to fit the space. This alone will help you narrow the choices.

Before selecting a shrub, determine how you want to use it in your garden. There are several factors to consider when choosing shrubs for both aesthetic and practical purposes.

Know the size constraints of your planting site and select a shrub accordingly. Common boxwoods are easily kept as a hedge with minimal pruning.

Shrubs that range from dwarf to treelike proportions provide the backbone for this courtyard.

A treelike Burford holly encloses a private sitting area.

Low Shrubs

Low-growing shrubs, which mature at less than 30 inches tall, are especially useful in front of low windows and as ground covers. They can also serve as a permanent planting on sloping ground that is too steep to mow. Low shrubs may be the primary plants for confined gardens, such as a courtyard. Examples are the low, spreading cotoneasters and Gumpo azaleas.

Medium Shrubs

The medium-sized shrubs, which measure from 2½ to 6 feet tall, are the largest and most diverse category. This group includes Helleri holly, Rotunda holly, many boxwoods, and dwarf forms of larger plants, such as yaupon holly. You can use medium shrubs for hedges, low screens, or foundation plantings. Sprawling shrubs, such as spireas, can even be used as ground covers over large banks and areas that are difficult to mow or cultivate. Shrubs in this size range remain manageable and often provide a sense of separation along a patio or terrace without completely enclosing the setting.

Large Shrubs

Large shrubs grow more than 6 feet tall and generally as wide. Ligustrum, wax myrtle, rhododendron, and common boxwood are evergreen stalwarts of this group. Forsythia, native azaleas, flowering quince, and hydrangea are among their deciduous counterparts.

Large shrubs do most of the shaping and screening in the landscape. Use them to establish privacy, screen unwanted views, or anchor and frame a large design. Give them room to grow; a healthy forsythia will ultimately reach the size of a small car. Use this mental image to remember the space that large shrubs require.

Some large shrubs, such as wax myrtle and Burford holly, grow tall quickly. Remove the lower branches to turn them into small trees. This is a handsome way to "recycle" shrubs for a new use.

Form

A shrub's form is a factor in the landscape throughout the year. When carefully chosen, shrubs provide the main interest in a garden, especially when few plants are in bloom. Planting a variety of forms results in an overall design that is greater than the sum of its parts.

Plant a cushion form, such as Helleri holly, before a backdrop with an upright, fountain form, such as nandina. In a similar fashion, the spreading form of Wheeler's dwarf pittosporum planted in front of upright, oval wax myrtle makes a statement of contrast among plant forms.

Below are descriptions of some common shrub forms and how they may be best used in the garden.

• **Upright, oval.** This is the largest and most varied group of shrubs. These plants are taller than they are broad and are excellent for creating living garden walls and defining space within the garden. Examples are camellia, wax myrtle, and common boxwood.

• **Spreading.** These shrubs are usually wider than they are tall and have a horizontal branching pattern; they often spread by underground shoots. Harbor Dwarf nandina, for example, is an excellent ground cover on a sloping site or beneath existing trees.

• **Upright.** These shrubs are very architectural in form and usage. Plant them as vertical accents. Leatherleaf mahonia is an example.

• **Fountain or weeping.** This is an unusual, eye-catching form. Weeping yaupon is one such plant; it makes a handsome backdrop for contrasting forms and also has sufficient grace to be an effective accent.

• **Rounded or mounding.** This dependable form is the staple of foundation plantings. Dwarf boxwood is the best known of the rounded group; a lovely mounding shrub is oakleaf hydrangea.

• **Cushion.** Some shrubs, such as Helleri holly, have a compact, neat form. These are useful in foundation plantings.

• **Matting.** These shrubs spread like rugs across the garden. Bearberry cotoneaster is an example. Matting shrubs are best used as ground covers, either planted in place of grass or to prevent erosion.

Sun or Shade?

You should know the hours of direct sun that a given spot in your garden will receive in order to wisely select a shrub for it. This knowledge is acquired through a bit of observation and is essential for proper planting. If you have no trees on your lot, you should pick shrubs that thrive in full sun. Similarly, if your lot has a continuous

Combining rounded and spreading forms makes an entry memorable.

The fountain form of Reeves spirea is most evident when the shrub is in bloom.

A large lot usually has a variety of exposures; you must select plants with their sun or shade requirements in mind.

tree canopy, look to the shade-loving plants. If you have a lot with both sun and shade, you must pay close attention to potential planting locations. Understanding the light conditions in your landscape is one of the finer points of gardening.

• **Beware of afternoon sun.** During the growing season, direct sun is most intense between 11:00 A.M. and 3:00 P.M., causing heat to build up and the temperature to peak around 4:00 P.M. This is particularly true after the adjustment to daylight savings time. Direct sun during these hours is so intense that you should consider any spot receiving it a full-sun location. If a spot receives sun from 1:00 P.M. to sunset or is at the foundation of a south- or southwest-facing wall it will also be a full-sun location; expect these sites to be very hot and dry during summer. These spots will also be warmer in winter because of the reflected sunlight; this may encourage shrubs to start growing too early in spring, making the tender new growth vulnerable to spring freezes.

You should shield any shade-loving plants from sun between 11:00 A.M. and 3:00 P.M., particularly from Zone 7 southward. Exceptions are the high elevations of the mountains, planting sites in the upper South that face north, or other areas where the overhead sun is less severe.

• **Know the value of morning sun.** You will find that there is some flexibility with plants that are designated for shade and partial shade. Most plants so labeled—aucuba and azaleas, for instance—will thrive with full sun until 11:00 A.M. during the growing season. Many experienced gardeners consider this time period the ideal sun exposure;

it provides sufficient light to keep plants full, helps set buds on flowering shrubs, and dries off moisture from humid nights but it is not so hot that it burns shade-loving plants. However, you should be aware that morning sun in winter may burn the foliage of evergreens, as their foliage may be frozen or coated in ice during a cold snap.

• **The sun varies in different parts of the country.** This is particularly true if you move from northern locations into the South. From Tennessee southward, the summer sun can devastate shrubs. Many plants grown in full sun in New England must be tucked away in the shade during midday in the South. Ask for advice at a local nursery or carefully observe local horticultural practices before planting.

Purchasing Shrubs

When buying shrubs at a nursery, common sense tells you to buy the selections that look good. Choose shrubs with robust, uniform color of both flowers and foliage—no dead, withered, or broken twigs or branches, and no droopy or withered foliage. Check that there are no insects, such as spider mites and scales, on the leaves and stems. Be sure that there are no leaf spots or other signs of disease and that the soil around the plant is firm, not dry or crumbly. Weeds growing in the container with the plant may be a sign of neglect or that the plant has been around for several seasons.

Shrubs for sale may be packaged in one of three ways: balled and burlapped, container grown, or bare root. Below is an explanation of each as well as some guidelines for handling plants.

Balled-and-Burlapped Shrubs

A good time to buy a balled-and-burlapped shrub is in midspring, when the leaves have emerged, so that there is no question about the plant's viability. However, if you buy from a reputable source that will guarantee its plants, buy a balled-and-burlapped plant in the fall so that the roots will have a chance to regenerate before new growth makes demands in the spring.

Container-Grown Shrubs

Container-grown shrubs are the most common; typically the plants are grown, shipped, and sold in black plastic containers that range from 1 to 10 gallons. Container-grown plants may be planted at any time of year, even summer if kept well watered.

Shrubs grown in containers are generally young and vigorous and have root systems proportionate to their size. Remember that bigger is not always better; a 16-inch-tall container-grown plant will likely grow at a faster rate than a 4-foot-tall balled-and-burlapped shrub, rapidly narrowing the gap between their sizes.

Pick a size that you can handle. Choose the healthiest specimen of the size you have chosen, but unless you have a pressing landscape need that requires very large shrubs immediately, stick to moderate-sized, container-grown nursery stock.

Bare-Root Shrubs

You may find shrubs sold as bare-root plants in late winter. These are plants that have no soil around their roots and are packed in moist sawdust or another material to preserve moisture. Check plants for signs of drying before you buy; stems should be firm and pliable.

Soak the roots in a bucket of water for a few hours before planting and then plant right away.

Handle with Care

To avoid causing injury to a shrub, always lift it by the root ball. If you lift the shrub by the trunk, the weight of the soil may tear the feeder roots. Roll a large plant onto an old sheet to make a sling for two people to grasp.

Wrap the shrub in burlap or an old sheet. When loading shrubs onto a truck, lay the foliage next to the cab to shield the leaves from the wind. Do not set the plants upright; the wind will tear the leaves and dry out green tissue.

Plant the shrub immediately or set it upright in a shady place and keep the roots moist and mulched until you can plant. Do not let it sit for more than a week or two without plenty of water. Be sure to protect the roots from direct sun or freezing weather.

Planting and Care

While many time-saving techniques are useful in gardening, there are no shortcuts for proper planting. Everything you can do to the ground to make it easier for your shrubs to grow will be time and effort well spent. This is true regardless of whether you are planting a single shrub, a privacy hedge along a property line, or an entire bed. The size of the planting, the extent of your energy, and the available time will determine whether you should rent a tiller or simply prepare the bed by hand.

Always Do a Soil Test

A soil test will assess your soil's chemistry. Is the acidity (pH) high or low? Does it lack crucial elements or is there an excess? A proper balance in the basic soil chemistry is essential for the growth of healthy plants; growth will be stunted if any nutrients are low or missing. A soil test will tell you what your soil needs.

Soil test kits are available through your county Agricultural Extension Service office. The kit contains directions for testing, along with a form to record your findings.

Preparing the Planting Bed

The ideal soil is loose enough to allow roots to expand easily. It is porous and well drained, yet able to retain moisture and nutrients. This is rare earth indeed around most homes; you will probably need to create your own by adding wheelbarrow loads of organic matter, such as sphagnum peat moss, compost, or manure, to the existing soil. Organic matter improves clay soil by breaking up the texture, opening it up so that roots can breathe and drain. In poor, sandy soil organic matter helps retain moisture and nutrients.

You may hear that some plants grow well without soil amendments; this applies only when respectable topsoil is present. In many areas, the topsoil has eroded or construction has left whole neighborhoods sitting on rock-hard subsoil; breaking up the ground and adding amendments throughout the bed will help ensure that your plants will grow. Remember, the nursery-grown plants you purchase have been growing in an ideal, friable soil. They will not make a good transition into the hard subsoil found around many homes.

When possible, begin preparing your soil a couple of weeks before planting so that you can do the job in manageable stages rather than all at once.

Once you have selected your plants, the next step toward establishing shrubs in your garden is preparing the soil.

Properly planted, a small shrub, such as this modest camellia, will live longer and grow faster.

Remove Any Vegetation

If the spot has never been cultivated, begin by removing anything growing there. You can transplant healthy grass to bare spots elsewhere in the yard or spray the entire area with a nonselective herbicide (a grass and weed killer) to kill vegetation. (Remember that these products will kill everything green that they touch, so follow label directions carefully.) In a week to ten days you can break up the dead vegetation with a turning fork or tiller, rake it out, and remove it to a compost pile.

Work the Soil

Use a turning fork or tiller to work the soil as deeply as possible, preferably 12 to 18 inches in heavy clay. Spread a layer of organic matter 3 to 4 inches deep over the area and work this until well blended with your native soil. Continue working the mix until it aggregates in pieces no larger than a quarter. Pulverized pine bark, which is often sold in bags labeled "soil conditioner," is an effective and inexpensive soil amendment.

You can modify this technique by concentrating your resources. For example, if you are planting a privacy hedge along a property line, till a continuous bed at least 4 feet wide the entire planting length. This will give you a mowing edge to maintain, which is easier than mowing between individual plants. Then, when you spread organic matter, spread the greatest amount in a 2- to 3-foot circle in the exact location for each shrub instead of evenly distributing it throughout the bed.

Planting

You cannot dig a hole too wide for a shrub; bigger is always better as far as the area for root expansion is concerned. A carefully prepared bed helps ensure that the roots will spread through the top 8 to 12 inches of soil. The development of a good root system is essential to the health and vigor of a shrub.

If you are planting a single shrub, dig a hole at least twice as wide (preferably three to five times as large) but no deeper than the root ball. Take the edge of a shovel and slice into the sides of the hole—the looser this soil, the easier it will be for roots to penetrate.

When planting multiple shrubs, set all of them in their holes before backfilling. If you need to make an adjustment, you do not have to dig up the plants.

Spacing Shrubs

Proper spacing ensures that your plants will grow well and do what you selected them to do. Here are some tips to help you develop a healthy garden.

• When planting a large bed, place plants at the recommended spacing in a diamond grid pattern, so that any three plants are equidistant from each other.

• Do not plant a shrub that will grow taller than 30 inches beside the driveway at the street. You must be able to see over the planting for safety.

• You will be tempted to space plants too closely when plants are small. Remember that they will close the gap. Adhere to the recommended spacing so that the plants can reach their maximum size without crowding.

Balled-and-Burlapped Shrubs

When you plant a balled-and-burlapped shrub, set the plant in the hole so that the top of the root ball is level with or sits an inch or two above the top of the hole. When the plant is at the proper height, peel back the burlap, folding it down the sides of the root ball.

Never remove the burlap from the plant; it helps keep the root ball intact and will decompose after planting. However, you should unfasten the burlap at the top of the root ball and fold it down from the top to be sure that it does not protrude above ground after planting. If the burlap is exposed to the surface, it will act as a wick to draw moisture away from the root ball. While roots will easily grow through cotton burlap, synthetic burlap must be split with a knife after the plant is in place to allow the roots to break through. Make three or four vertical slices through the material before refilling the hole.

Refill the hole with soil, mounding it over the sides of the exposed root ball, and water thoroughly.

Container-Grown Shrubs

Plant a container-grown shrub the same way you would a balled-and-burlapped plant, digging a hole no deeper than the root ball. The best way to remove the plant from the container is to turn the plant upside

Although you will be tempted to plant closely, adhere to the recommended spacing.

HINTS FOR BREAKING NEW GROUND

• When testing your soil, take samples from different parts of the proposed bed to get an accurate reading.

• Mark the outline of a new bed with a garden hose or draw the proposed perimeter of the bed with spray paint. Check the outline of the bed with your lawnmower to make sure it will not be difficult to mow around.

• Never work the soil when it is wet, as it will dry in clods. But tilling is easier if the soil is slightly moist, especially heavy clay soil. Water the day before tilling, or plan your project to follow a light rain.

Mulch reduces the need for watering and helps keep down weeds. Organic mulch, such as pine straw or bark, will also improve the soil as it decomposes.

WHEN SOIL DOES NOT DRAIN WELL

When planting in poorly drained areas, you may plant "on top" of the ground. This technique works well for azaleas and other shrubs that do not like soggy soil. After preparing the bed, dig the planting hole so shallow that the top half to three-fourths of the root ball sits above ground. Cover the root ball by mounding soil over it. Mulch with a 2- to 3-inch layer of pine bark and keep the area watered. For best results, plant in groups and mound the entire area.

down and let it slip out of the container. If roots have grown through the drainage holes, you will have to break them off. Cut away the pot with hand shears if necessary.

If the plant is too large to hold upside down, place it on its side on the ground so that you can pull the container from the roots. Avoid pulling and yanking the base of the shrub as you may tear feeder roots. Whenever possible, remove the container from the shrub, not the shrub from the container.

If the roots are matted and tangled, spread them out by cutting crosswise through the bottom third of the root ball, making sure no large roots grow in a circle around the plant.

Mulching

In summer, mulch helps keep the roots cool; in winter, it helps prevent alternate freezing and thawing that can heave fall-planted shrubs. Mulch also helps conserve moisture and keeps down weeds.

Give shrubs a 3-inch layer of organic mulch, such as shredded bark or pine straw. When planting several shrubs, mulch the entire bed.

Watering

The single most important thing you can do to ensure the success of a new planting is to keep it watered. Water each plant gently (not at full pressure) at the base for a few minutes so that the water penetrates the planting hole. Be sure to water at the base of the plant; a small sprinkler or a sprinkler system may not deliver adequate water to a newly planted shrub where the water is most needed. Later, as the shrubs expand into the larger growing area, a sprinkler will be adequate for watering.

It is better to water deeply just once a week than to give plants a shallow watering more often. To deliver a deep watering, you should apply about an inch of water at a time. Measure this by setting a rain gauge or small can under the sprinkler (place pans under soaker hoses); when the water is an inch deep, you can turn off the spigot. If you note how long it takes to deliver an inch of water, you can set a timer on your spigot or automatic irrigation system to deliver the right amount every time.

How often you water will depend upon your soil type and the temperature. Generally, once a week is enough, but in sandy soils that dry out faster you may need to water two or even three times a week during extremely hot, dry weather.

Fertilizing

Feeding with a slow-release tree-and-shrub fertilizer at the time of planting will give your shrubs a head start on developing a healthy root system. The roots will sustain the plant through varying environmental stresses.

When you buy a fertilizer, choose one that has at least 50 percent slow-release nitrogen. This type may seem more expensive, but in the long run it is not. You are paying for the gradual release of nitrogen, which stimulates new growth steadily over time. Fertilizers that do not contain slow-release nitrogen release all of their nitrogen quickly, rushing excessive nutrients into the soil only to have them washed away with the first heavy rain.

There are also many specialty fertilizer products that target specific shrub types, such as evergreens, azaleas, and flowering shrubs. Read the labels and compare the formulations to all-purpose slow-release fertilizers. Sometimes you may target a group of shrubs with similar needs; azaleas, gardenias, and camellias need extra iron to maintain a deep green foliage, for example. However, one universal tree-and-shrub food will serve most shrubs in your garden and makes fertilizing a lot simpler.

You may consider an initial fertilization with a liquid root stimulant. Such a product will provide a needed boost during the critical first few weeks after planting.

You may also "push" shrubs into quick growth by giving them a liquid plant food every few weeks, especially in spring. Spraying the liquid food directly on the foliage allows it to be absorbed more quickly than in-ground feeding.

Spring is a good time to fertilize because plants are growing rapidly. Generally, you should fertilize early in spring to take advantage of the full season of growth. While spring feeding is typical, many shrubs also benefit from a fall feeding immediately after the first killing frost. Feeding after a hard frost with a formula low in nitrogen, such as a winterizer product, will provide nutrients to the roots without enticing new growth. (You do not want to encourage any new growth at this time.)

This late-fall feeding is very important in the South, where soil temperatures are still warm enough for roots to grow and store nutrients. After the ground cools, this fertilizer will remain inactive until spring, when growth resumes.

WHAT IS A SLOW-RELEASE FERTILIZER?

Slow-release fertilizer is sometimes called *controlled-release* because it releases small amounts of nutrients at a time. The nutrients are coated and held in reserve to be delivered gradually over several weeks or months, depending on soil moisture and temperature.

The label will indicate whether the fertilizer contains slow-release nitrogen. There is a wide price range depending on the percentage of coated nitrogen and other nutrients a fertilizer contains. Look for one that includes at least 50 percent slow-release nitrogen.

Pruning

Prune shrubs only slightly to improve their looks, health, and growth or to maintain them in a clipped form. If you find yourself pruning because a shrub is in your way, remove the shrub and start again.

Except in the cases of clipped hedges, espaliered shrubs, or other artful forms, pruning should be an occasional chore that helps maintain the garden's visual balance and the health of the shrub. A few shrubs, such as nandina and abelia, benefit from periodic shaping that allows the shrub to rejuvenate its form by replacing the old woody growth with newer, more vigorous shoots. This is the horticultural equivalent of a hair trim. Generally, you should not have to prune a shrub much, if at all. If you find yourself fighting shrubs because they are too tall or too wide, they are planted in the wrong place. In the long run, replacing them with shrubs of the proper size will save you both time and effort.

You can often salvage old, overgrown shrubs by pruning them. Decades-old forsythia and abelia can be restored by removing or cutting back the oldest (generally the thickest and tallest) canes to the ground. Remove the lower limbs of overgrown wax myrtles and Burford hollies to train them into small trees.

Reasons To Prune

Good reasons to prune a shrub are to thin it, to remove dead wood and awkward branches, and to shape the shrub into a hedge, espalier, or other deliberate form.

Thinning

Thinning means removing branches or shoots from the interior of the shrub to permit air and light to penetrate. Since it will also stimulate the plant to rejuvenate, this technique is sometimes called *renewal pruning.* If you thin properly, you may remove as much as one-third of the branches, taking the oldest branches first and making the shrub slightly smaller and less dense but still retaining its natural form. Unless the shrub is in deep shade, new growth will quickly begin to fill in. This technique is very useful for large forsythia, weigela, or fruitland elaeagnus.

Removing Dead Branches

Prune to remove dead branches, which can harbor harmful insects and promote disease. Timely pruning may allow you to prevent the spread of decay or disease into the rest of the shrub. Cut the branch back to healthy wood, preferably just above a bud.

This old, overgrown abelia hedge is given new life with renewal pruning.

Correcting Awkward Branching

Prune to remove any awkward or annoying branches. Crisscrossing branches in the shrub's interior may eventually rub against each other, causing open sores that are conduits for diseases and insect pests. This is particularly true with flowering quince, doublefile viburnum, and rockspray cotoneaster.

Shaping

Prune the tips of the stems to help plants grow more densely. Snip the center leaf bud to allow the side shoots of rhododendron to flourish; this also increases the spread of the plant. Wax myrtle will rapidly fill in thickly with tip pruning in spring; older boxwoods respond especially well to a deliberate thinning over a period of years that allows foliage to grow in the interior of the plant.

Finally, regular pruning is needed to maintain a hedge or espalier. A hedge is usually sheared, becoming architectural in character to form a low, green wall. You should prune hedge plantings before the new growth appears in the spring. See the box and illustrations on this page for guidelines on pruning a hedge to keep it full at the bottom.

Hedge 1 has been sheared straight up and down. Eventually, the lower branches die, like those of Hedge 2. Hedge 3 stays thick because its bottom is slightly wider than its top. Hedge 4 has been maintained as an informal screen.

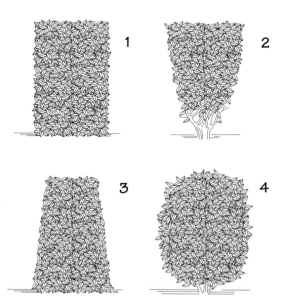

THE PROPER WAY TO PRUNE A HEDGE

The best formal hedges are trimmed from plants with small leaves, such as common boxwood, English boxwood, wax myrtle, and Japanese holly. When you prune plants with larger leaves, such as Burford holly, the edge of the cut will turn brown, making the plant unsightly.

Maintaining a formal hedge takes more than constant shearing; it also demands the correct technique. Do not make the mistake of trimming a hedge so that its sides are straight up and down or so that it is wider at the top than it is at the bottom. In both cases, the hedge's lower branches are shaded by the top of the hedge. When this happens, the bottom branches thin and die, leaving the hedge leggy and bare at ground level. To prevent this, shear the hedge so that it is slightly wider at the bottom than it is at the top. This will allow sunlight to reach the lower branches, keeping the foliage full at the base.

Plant Hardiness Zone Map

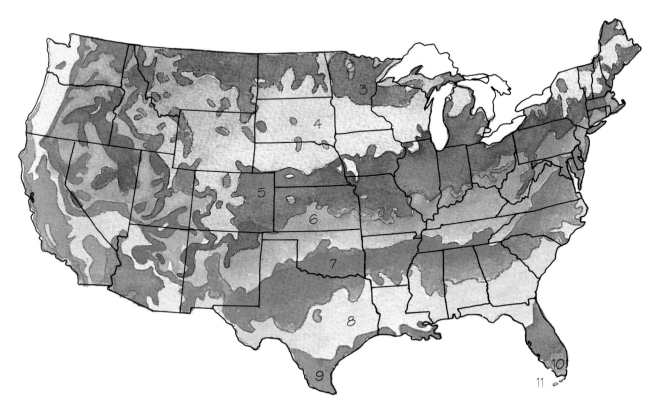

The United States Department of Agriculture has charted low temperatures throughout the country to determine the ranges of average low readings. The map above is based loosely on the USDA Plant Hardiness Zone Map, which was drawn from these findings. It does not take into account heat, soil, or moisture extremes and is intended as a guide, not a guarantee.

The southern regions of the United States that are mentioned in this book refer to the following:

Upper South: Zone 6
Middle South: upper region of Zone 7 (0 to 5 degrees minimum)
Lower South: lower region of Zone 7 and upper region of Zone 8 (5 to 15 degrees minimum)
Coastal South: lower region of Zone 8 and upper region of Zone 9 (15 to 25 degrees minimum)
Tropical South: lower region of Zone 9 and all of Zone 10 (25 to 40 degrees minimum)

Zone 2	-50	to	-40°F
Zone 3	-40	to	-30°F
Zone 4	-30	to	-20°F
Zone 5	-20	to	-10°F
Zone 6	-10	to	0°F
Zone 7	0	to	10°F
Zone 8	10	to	20°F
Zone 9	20	to	30°F
Zone 10	30	to	40°F
Zone 11		above	40°F

Shrub Profiles

The shrubs described in the following pages were selected by the garden editors at *Southern Living* for their availability, dependability, and many garden uses, which make them the most popular and reliable shrubs for successful landscaping. By choosing shrubs carefully you can add color, fragrance, and texture to your garden as well as provide a framework of design.

Arranged alphabetically by common name, these profiles give you a description of each shrub, information about planting and care, and suggested ways that you can incorporate its color, height, and form into your garden. Critical to your success is knowing the soil and cultural conditions each shrub needs; this information, as well as troubleshooting tips and solutions, is contained in the profiles.

When a genus contains more than one species, such as the azaleas, the group is contained in a single entry. The profile points out the differences in appearance and growing needs of the most popular species within the group.

For a quick overview of the shrub, refer to the *At a Glance* box that accompanies every profile. This will give you the major features of the shrub, including its botanical name to help you avoid confusion when buying plants.

Shrubs are important elements in the landscape. Their successful growth depends upon your care and maintenance; with proper conditions, the right shrubs will enhance both your garden and your home for years to come.

Dwarf winged euonymus

Abelia

Abelia blooms throughout summer.

Abelia is a durable evergreen that blooms with little attention in the brunt of summer heat. This tough shrub is sometimes called glossy abelia because of its glossy, dark green foliage. Its small but profuse white flowers appear in June and continue until frost. Butterflies are attracted to the blooms.

The plant has an airy, open growth habit. The branches are upright and arching, and the plant quickly grows to between 3 and 6 feet in both height and width, depending on the selection. The white, bell-shaped flowers are borne on the tips of young shoots.

The soft leaves are 1 to 1½ inches long and taper to a point, remaining a deep, glossy green during the growing season. In winter, they often turn slightly bronze. In colder areas of its range, abelia will shed its leaves or may be killed to the ground in winter but will quickly come back in spring.

In the Landscape

Abelia looks best as a loose privacy screen, especially in the middle South. It also works well beside a wall or a tall backdrop, such as ligustrum or Burford holly. Because of its small leaves, abelia may be trimmed as a hedge. However, it is best left alone, with occasional pruning to renew older growth. (See page 28 for more about renewal pruning.) Abelia will also serve as a good anchor in a large shrub border or foundation planting.

Planting and Care

Plant abelia in full sun or partial shade in moist, well-drained, slightly acid soil. Blooming is best when plants receive at least six hours of direct sunlight daily.

If you live in an area where the shrub is killed back in winter, simply remove the dead canes. The plant responds very well to pruning, and a well-established plant will fill out quickly as the weather warms in spring. You can reduce winter damage by planting abelia in an area that does not receive early morning sun and is protected from winter winds.

Species and Selections

Many selections of dwarf forms of abelia make good foundation plants and ground covers. Edward Goucher is valued for its pink flowers that appear from June until frost. Prostrata is a low-growing,

Abelia makes an excellent hedge to enclose a garden space, though it requires regular pruning to keep it tidy.

compact form with smaller leaves that grows only 3 to 4 feet tall; Sherwood is also a compact form with small leaves and grows to about 3 feet tall.

Abelia chinensis is a related species with larger blooms and leaves and grows taller than *Abelia* x *grandiflora*. It is prized for its fragrant blooms that appear in mid- to late summer and have an even greater attraction for butterflies than those of other abelias. However, it is less cold hardy, growing only from Zones 6 to 9.

Althea

Cedar Lane is an unusually colored selection with white petals and a red center.

AT A GLANCE
❖
ALTHEA
Hibiscus syriacus

Features: continuous summer flowers

Foliage: deciduous

Height: 8 to 12 feet

Width: 6 to 10 feet

Light: full sun to partial shade

Soil: moist, well drained

Water: moderate

Range: Zones 5 to 9

Pests: spider mites, Japanese beetles, whiteflies, leaf spot

Remarks: tolerant of poor soil conditions

When the heat of summer is unbearable, althea, also known as rose of Sharon, seems unstoppable, opening its large blooms atop a treelike shrub even in the hottest locations. Althea begins blooming as early as May in the deep South and continues through September or later.

Althea's large, 4- to 6-inch-wide flowers open at dawn and close in the evening. Their shape is similar to that of hibiscus blossoms; hibiscus and althea are closely related. But unlike hibiscus, each bloom lives more than one day.

Althea grows at a moderate rate to become an upright shrub between 8 and 12 feet tall and about 8 feet wide. The leaves have three lobes reminiscent of maple leaves and are 2 to 4 inches long. In fall, they drop from the shrub without much color, leaving a bare-branched, scruffy winter form. The upright, spreading growth habit makes it appear thin at the base; you may remove some of the lower branches to train it into a tree form or use it in a bed of medium-sized evergreen shrubs, such as Helleri holly or Indian hawthorn.

In the Landscape

Althea is an old-fashioned shrub that works well in a shrub border either alone or combined with other shrubs to create a summer screen. The plant also works well with traditional garden structures, such as a split-rail fence or a lattice trellis.

Because of its height and treelike form, althea may also be used as a freestanding specimen, especially in a rustic setting where its twiggy branches and unkempt winter form are best appreciated. In bloom, althea looks good against a dark backdrop of evergreens or woods or placed in front of an architectural feature, such as a fence, a wall, a porch, or an outbuilding.

Planting and Care

Althea grows in full sun or partial shade. It prefers moist, well-drained soil that has plenty of organic matter, but the shrub is also very tolerant of a variety of soils and planting conditions. It is a good plant for the warmer portions of its hardiness range.

The flowers appear on new growth, so any pruning for shape should be completed by early spring.

Different Selections

Although you will find many unnamed specimens of this old-fashioned plant, you will also find named selections for sale at garden centers, chosen for their variation in flower color or some other trait. The flowers of many seedling altheas are lavender pink. In fact, older selections will produce many leggy seedlings around the garden, but new hybrids, such as Aphrodite, Diana, Helene, and Minerva, do not.

Aphrodite is a selection that has deep, rose pink blooms with red centers. Cedar Lane's blooms have white petals with red centers. Diana has large, pure white blooms that remain open at night, making it a good choice for planting near patios and decks where it will show up under moonlight and night lighting. Helene also has white blooms with reddish-purple centers. Minerva has pinkish-lavender blooms with darker centers.

Troubleshooting

Althea is bothered by spider mites and Japanese beetles. Turn to pages 124-125 for more about these pests. Whiteflies may attack the shrub; it may also get leaf spot. None of these cause serious damage. The plant will outgrow most damage and thrives on neglect.

An upright, irregular shrub, althea may be used singly or as a deciduous screen.

Andromeda

The delicate-looking blooms of andromeda last for weeks.

AT A GLANCE
❖
ANDROMEDA
Pieris japonica

Features: exquisite foliage, delicate pearl-like strands of flowers

Foliage: evergreen

Height: 3 to 12 feet

Width: 4 to 6 feet

Light: partial shade

Soil: moist, well drained, slightly acid, rich

Water: moderate

Range: Zones 5 to 8

Pests: lacebugs

Remarks: a good sculptural accent

With evergreen foliage and a wandering, slightly unpredictable, upright growth habit, andromeda brings an individual style to the garden that defies duplication. Also called Japanese andromeda or pieris, the plant is very stately and grows slowly to become a living landscape sculpture. When mature, andromeda can reach 12 feet in height and 4 to 6 feet in width.

From late summer throughout the entire winter, delicate pale green chains of flower buds hang daintily from the ends of the stems. These early-forming panicles are precursors to the upcoming blooms. In early spring, these tiny blooms open to drape the entire plant in exquisite 3- to 6-inch-long strands of cupped flowers. These are an extraordinary contrast to the handsome whorls of deep green leaves. The flowers are waxy and the pearly strands may last a month or more, since they appear when the weather is still very cool.

When in bloom, andromeda looks as if it were showered with pearls. Following bloom is a bronze-colored surge of new growth that quickly turns deep green. By the end of summer, the next season's panicles appear and the cycle starts anew.

In the Landscape

The intriguing form and attractive flowering habits of andromeda are at home in most garden styles. It is beautiful in a naturalistic setting with rhododendrons or azaleas, or you may set it in a glade of ferns as a specimen plant. Because of its sculptural form, andromeda also serves well as an accent plant; place it beside an entry or a garden statue. However, mass plantings of andromeda seem less effective in the landscape. Reserve this excellent evergreen for use as a single, prominent specimen.

Planting and Care

Andromeda is hardy from Zones 5 to 8. Plant it in moist, well-drained, acid soil in partial shade in the southern part of its range. It will do well in full sun in Zone 5, although it may need shelter from winter winds. Because it is relatively cold hardy, it is a good choice for year-round evergreen foliage in a container, but you must keep it in shade; do not let its thin, hairlike roots dry out.

Species and Selections

Mountain pieris *(Pieris floribunda)* is a low, spreading evergreen (2 to 6 feet tall) that likes rocky, acid soil and is native to the United

States. There are numerous selections with pink flowers; Mountain Fire has striking, bright red new growth and tolerates more direct sun than other selections. Pygmaea has tiny, narrow, feathery leaves and grows only 3 to 4 feet tall. Variegata has leaves with white margins and may grow to 10 feet. White Cascade has long panicles of pure white flowers. Compacta is a small, compact form that blooms profusely and grows 3 to 4 feet tall.

Troubleshooting

Andromeda is susceptible to lacebugs, which can be very damaging. See page 125 for more about lacebugs. Mountain pieris is not as susceptible to this pest.

Andromeda is a dense mass of green in the summer.

Andromeda seems to drip with pearls in early spring.

Aucuba

Picturata is one of the brightest selections of aucuba.

AT A GLANCE

❖

AUCUBA
Aucuba japonica

Features: glossy foliage, upright form
Foliage: evergreen
Height: 3 to 10 feet
Width: 2 to 3 feet
Light: partial shade to deep shade
Soil: moist, well drained
Water: moderate
Range: Zones 7 to 10
Pests: sclerotinia leaf fungus
Remarks: a dependable choice for deep shade

The large, coarse-textured leaves are one hallmark of this upright shrub; the other is that it will stay full and handsome even in shade. If you plant aucuba under the canopy of trees or on the north side of a structure, it will provide a lush, tropical look that brightens dark corners.

Sometimes called Japanese aucuba, this shrub may remind you of a houseplant because of its large leaves and bold texture. The species has dark green glossy leaves that are as much as 8 inches in length. Shrubs may reach 10 feet in height but can be kept at half that height if the tallest branches are selectively pruned in late winter. Generally, the plant keeps a very narrow, upright form but may grow wider in response to pruning. This shrub is *dioecious;* it bears male and female flowers on different plants. If male and female shrubs are planted together, cherry-sized bright red berries appear from October through winter on female plants.

In the Landscape

An irregular, multistemmed habit of growth makes aucuba a natural for informal plantings, while its dressy foliage allows its use in more formal settings. It can be used as an alternative to rhododendron in naturalistic plantings or as a foliage contrast with edging boxwood. It also works well in the narrow space between a house and a sidewalk or a driveway or as the accent plant in an enclosed entry or courtyard. The variegated selections have an even more exotic effect. Their brightly splotched leaves introduce light color to deep shade.

Planting and Care

Aucuba will remain thick in deep shade. You must protect it from direct overhead sunshine, which will burn the leaves. Plant it in sandy soil that is rich in organic matter, conditions very similar to those preferred by dogwood trees. This shrub likes well-drained soil; soggy conditions will kill it. In cold weather, its leaves curl up and seem to wilt, but they perk up as soon as the weather warms.

Different Selections

Although all aucubas may look alike at first, if you compare them carefully, you will notice many different patterns in the foliage. Leaves range from solid green to variegated, and many aucubas are not named selections. Crassifolia is a male plant with dark green foliage; Macrophylla is similar but female. Crotonifolia has large leaves that are finely speckled with yellow. Longifolia is a selection with narrow leaves; Nana, a compact form, grows about one-half the size of the species. Dwarf Green is a common selection with lance-shaped leaves. Variegata may be the most common selection, also called gold dust plant for the tiny gold spots on the dark green leaves. Mr. Goldstrike is a selection with more gold spots than Variegata, so it appears brighter in shade. Picturata has a solid yellow blotch in the middle of each leaf surrounded by smaller yellow flecks.

Troubleshooting

Although aucuba is usually a pest-free plant, sclerotinia leaf fungus can cause the leaves to turn black and the stems to die back. Before purchasing plants, check with your county Extension agent to find out if this problem is prevalent in your area.

Variegated aucuba brightens a shady area and contrasts with the deep green foliage of English ivy.

This green-leafed aucuba is a dressy foliage plant for deeply shaded sites.

Cherry-sized bright red fruit will appear on female plants if male plants grow nearby.

Azalea

Plumleaf azalea is a rare native azalea.

Azaleas, the most popular shrubs in the South, are staples of springtime color. They can be classified in two main groups: deciduous and evergreen. Their uses and forms vary greatly, so be sure to consider their differences when planning your landscape.

Deciduous Azaleas

The deciduous azaleas, sometimes called native azaleas or wild honeysuckle, are twiggy, wandering shrubs that may be the size of a small tree. They bring fragrant blooms of white, pink, lilac, orange, red, and even yellow into the garden. The flowers appear in clusters borne at the ends of the branches and may emerge before or after the foliage, depending on the species.

By carefully planning before you plant, you may have a mix of these handsome shrubs in bloom from early spring to late summer.

In the Landscape

In the wild, deciduous azaleas are most often found at the edge of a wooded area or in a clearing—a clue to their best use in the home landscape. In such locations, the branches seem to emerge in an irregular tangle that almost disappears into the backdrop of woods. When the plants bloom, the flowers seem to be suspended above the ground; this is especially true of species that bloom before their leaves emerge.

Plant these shrubs at the edge of a naturalistic border or tuck them beneath the canopy of a grouping of trees. A neutral backdrop, such as a fence or a wall, will silhouette both the flowers and the form of the plant.

Plant deciduous azaleas in an out-of-the-way border where they will bloom and then fade from view, or take advantage of their form by planting them in the center of a courtyard or in a planter beside an entry. Because of their grace and sculptural quality, deciduous azaleas also work as specimens in a small garden, even if the overall design is more formal.

A deciduous azalea is an excellent choice for a linear accent among evergreen azaleas, serving as a counterpoint to the mounding form of evergreen selections. They also work well with rhododendrons and andromeda, two shade-loving evergreens. When planted singly or in a drift, the plants are a handsome show of blooms beneath the canopy of tall pines or hardwoods.

AT A GLANCE

❖

DECIDUOUS AZALEAS
Azalea species

Features: spectacular flowers and fall color, twiggy form

Foliage: deciduous

Height: 4 to 15 feet

Width: 3 to 10 feet

Light: light shade

Soil: rich, acid, well drained

Water: moderate

Range: Zones 5 to 9

Pests: none specific

Remarks: durable, elegant shrubs

Planting and Care

Once established, most deciduous azaleas are tough and durable. Direct morning sun will help the plants set buds; shelter them from the blistering midday summer sun. In deep shade, these shrubs will not flower as profusely as they will in at least partial sun.

Deciduous azaleas prefer acid, rich, loose soil that is moist yet well drained. Mulch the plants with chopped leaves or pine straw to keep the soil moist. This is critical as deciduous azaleas have shallow, fibrous root systems that can dry out easily.

Different Species

Most of these species of deciduous azaleas are native to the Eastern United States and are adaptable throughout the country; check with a local source for the adaptability of a particular species to your area. Plants marked with an asterisk (*) have fragrant flowers.

Alabama azalea* *(Azalea alabamense)* is a native shrub with fragrant flowers, usually white with a yellow throat, that open about the time the leaves emerge. It grows 3 to 6 feet tall.

Coast azalea* *(Azalea atlanticum)* is also native and has flowers that vary from white to pink. It may grow to 6 feet, though it is usually not that tall. The foliage is bluish green. It is found along the coastal woodlands from Delaware southward.

Flame azalea *(Azalea calendulaceum)* bears large blooms that vary from brilliant red to orange to yellow. These are large plants, growing to 8 feet tall and spreading to 10 feet, that bloom from mid-May to late June. These shrubs are hardy from Pennsylvania to Georgia.

Florida flame azalea* *(Azalea austrinum)* has fragrant flowers that vary from golden yellow to soft orange and appear in spring, before the leaves. The plant may grow to 6 feet tall and thrives as far south as north Florida.

Oconee azalea *(Azalea flammeum)* has flowers that vary from orange to red to pink. This azalea grows to about 6 feet and the flowers generally appear as the leaves unfold.

Piedmont azalea* *(Azalea canescens)* has fragrant flowers that range from white to deep pink. It is almost treelike in stature, often growing to 15 feet tall. The most abundant azalea species in the South, it blooms before or with new leaves.

The bright yellow-orange flowers of this Florida flame azalea show the soft, airy quality of deciduous azaleas.

A close look at this Pinxterbloom azalea flower reveals its delicate structure.

Pinxterbloom azalea* *(Azalea periclymenoides)* also has fragrant flowers, which vary from white to pale pink to violet. Blooms open before the leaves appear. Plants grow to about 6 feet in height. This cold-hardy azalea does not like hot weather and grows best from Zones 4 to 8.

Plumleaf azalea *(Azalea prunifolium)* is prized for its late bloom; the red to orange-red flowers of this species are a surprise in July or August. It is a handsome shrub that may grow to 10 feet tall.

Swamp azalea* *(Azalea viscosum)* produces white to creamy white flowers in early summer, another nice change from spring blooms. The plants are a bit fuller than most deciduous azaleas and grow to about 5 feet tall. Swamp azalea is a better choice than other natives for soils that do not drain well.

Sweet azalea* *(Azalea arborescens)* has fragrant white blooms that are accented by pink central filaments. It grows to a treelike 20 feet and is hardy from Pennsylvania to Georgia.

Troubleshooting

With proper planting and care, most deciduous azaleas escape disease and pest difficulties.

Piedmont azalea is one of the most common native azaleas.

Evergreen Azaleas

If a single group of shrubs says spring, it is the evergreen azaleas. When they bloom, the landscape is covered in bouquets of countless shades of pink, red, purple, orange, and white.

While most gardeners immediately fall in love with evergreen azaleas for their blooms, you will grow to appreciate their longevity as well, once they are well established.

In the Landscape

Evergreen azaleas are most effective when used in drifts of separate colors that create a sweep of blooms. Their loose, irregular growth habit lends them to casual drifts instead of rigid, ordered beds. Solitary azaleas placed in borders are effective for splashes of color but not necessarily as accent plantings. Most azalea selections do not carry sufficient appeal throughout the year to justify use as specimen plants in highly prominent locations. Plant them so that you may enjoy their two weeks of spring glory, and then allow them to spend the remaining months in reserve.

You may enjoy evergreen azaleas for six weeks or more if you plant selections that bloom at different times during the season.

Planting and Care

Plant evergreen azaleas in partial shade; the filtered shade from tall pine trees or willow oaks is ideal. The plants will thrive in direct morning sun. Azaleas will tolerate full sun, but their shape becomes unnaturally dense, their foliage bleaches to yellow green, and they are more susceptible to lacebugs. In deep shade, evergreen azaleas may not bloom profusely, and the plants will become more open or even leggy in form as they reach for light.

Evergreen azaleas must have rich, loose soil that is moist yet well drained. In areas that have heavy clay soils, it is sometimes recommended to plant "on top" of the ground, so that the top half of the root ball is actually above ground level. Backfill to cover the exposed sides of the root ball.

Azaleas must have slightly acid soil; they will not grow in alkaline soil. If the water in your area is alkaline, you should monitor your soil pH and maintain the acid conditions needed by adding sulfur and acid-forming azalea fertilizer.

Red Ruffles is a Rutherford hybrid that does best in the lower South.

AT A GLANCE

❖

EVERGREEN AZALEAS
Azalea species and hybrids

Features: spring blossoms, reliable growth

Foliage: evergreen

Height: 3 to 10 feet

Width: 3 to 10 feet

Light: partial shade

Soil: rich, acid, moist, well drained

Water: moderate

Range: Zones 5 to 9

Pests: lacebugs, leaf miners, petal blight

Remarks: indispensable for spring blooms

Stone steps become a dominant garden feature when flanked by red azaleas.

One of the loveliest of the soft pinks is Fashion, a Glenn Dale hybrid.

Different Selections

The azaleas for sale in your area are typically the ones that sell best and are proven for your horticultural conditions. The following are the most popular groups of azaleas.

Back Acre hybrids do well in the coastal South. The young plants are not cold hardy, but those that are well established will survive winters in the lower and middle South. Marian Lee has a white center and a dark pink border.

Carla hybrids were bred at North Carolina State University and include Adelaine Pope, Pink Cloud, and Sunglow.

Gable hybrids were developed in Pennsylvania and are among the hardiest evergreen azaleas, tolerating temperatures as low as 20 degrees below zero. Stewartsonian is a popular orange selection.

Girard hybrids were bred for cold climates by Girard Nurseries in Geneva, Ohio. The flower buds are hardy to 5 degrees below zero or colder, and the plants are even more cold tolerant. All have Girard in their name, such as Girard's Scarlet and Girard Pink Delight.

Glenn Dale hybrids are a large group that varies in size and color; most are hardy to zero degrees. Ben Morrison has striking orange-red blooms with white margins. Martha Hitchcock has white flowers with purple margins and is one of the most popular azaleas.

Harris hybrids were developed in Lawrenceville, Georgia, have very large flowers, and are best suited to the deep South. Pink Cascade will spill over the edge of a wall or container.

Kurume hybrids bloom early in a wide range of colors. They require protection in Zone 7 during extreme cold. Selections include Coral Bells and Hino Crimson.

Mucronatum is a form of azalea that is popular in Japan and is sometimes sold as a species, *Rhododendron mucronatum*. Delaware Valley White (fragrant) is one of the hardiest and best white azaleas; others include Fielder's White and Indica Alba.

North Tisbury azaleas were developed on Martha's Vineyard, Massachusetts, and are prized for their cold hardiness (5 to 10 degrees below zero), late blooms, and low, spreading habit. Wintergreen is a dwarf, spreading plant with red flowers.

Among the hardiest azaleas are *Rhododendron kaempferi* and hybrids. Blooms are orange, red, pink, or purple; some selections bloom in May. These shrubs are hard to find.

Robin Hill hybrids were developed in New Jersey and are hardy to 10 degrees below zero. They are late bloomers but may bloom out of season in the lower South. Hilda Niblett is one of the most popular selections and has large pink flowers with dark red blotches. Gwenda often blooms again in the fall in the lower South.

Rutherford hybrids are bred mostly for the florist trade but will do well outdoors in Florida or the lower South. Dorothy Gish is a well-known orange-red selection.

Satsuki hybrids are low-growing, late-blooming azaleas that often need winter protection north of Zone 8. The most popular selections are Gumpos, which come in rose, pink, and white. Others have Japanese names, such as Wakebisu, Eikan, and Shinnyo-No-Tsuki.

Shammarello hybrids were developed in Ohio and are among the hardiest azaleas. Elsie Lee is a popular lavender; Hino Red (not to be confused with Hino Crimson, a parent) is another.

Southern Indian hybrids are the largest and most popular azaleas for the lower and coastal South. George Lindley Taber and Mrs. G.G. Gerbing are two cold-hardy selections, thriving as far north as coastal Virginia.

Troubleshooting

Evergreen azaleas may be bothered by lacebugs. Leaf miners may also form tunnels through the leaf tissue and render the plant unsightly, but they rarely cause severe damage. See page 125 for more about these pests. In a wet spring, a fungus called petal blight may also attack the flowers, turning the season's show to brown.

A TALE OF TWO AZALEAS

Southern Indian hybrid azaleas have a mounding growth habit and produce magnificent flowers. In the lower and coastal South they may soar tall enough to be good privacy hedges or screen plantings. They represent the best of what evergreen azaleas have to offer—extraordinary blooms on a graceful form.

The Satsuki hybrids, on the other hand, are ground-hugging shrubs that spread to 3 or 4 feet in width and grow to about 3 feet in height. Within this group are the popular Gumpo azaleas, handsome plants that bloom in May or early June. One bonus of this group is their handsome foliage throughout the year. Unlike most azaleas they have a high tolerance for direct sun, making them good ground covers and container plants.

Satsuki hybrids, which include the late-blooming Gumpo azaleas, extend the season for azaleas.

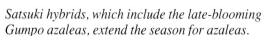

George Lindley Taber is one of the largest evergreen azaleas.

Barberry

Wintergreen barberry has spiny leaves.

A close inspection of this moderately fast-growing evergreen shrub reveals sharp spines along a dense network of twiggy branches. Do not dismiss it because of its armor; its handsome foliage, flowers, and fruit are attractive in every season.

Wintergreen Barberry

Wintergreen barberry grows as wide as it does tall. It is covered with lustrous, dark green, evergreen leaves that are 1 to 3 inches long with spiny, toothed edges. The foliage blushes wine red with frost in autumn and remains that color through winter.

Clusters of bright yellow flowers appear in spring in a modest but noticeable show. They are followed by dark blue fruits that ripen in summer and last through fall.

In the Landscape

Wintergreen barberry makes a superior informal hedge but is not as good as a trimmed hedge, as trimming ruins its twiggy form. It is also unmatched

Wintergreen barberry's waxy blue fruit is borne in clusters.

for barrier plantings. In spite of the spines, wintergreen barberry is handsome enough for foundation plantings or massed in poor, dry areas.

Planting and Care

Hardy in Zones 5 to 8, wintergreen barberry should be planted in full or partial sun in well-drained, slightly acid soil. Once established, the plant is very drought tolerant. This shrub is susceptible to winter windburn in Zone 5, and it struggles in the heat and humidity of the coastal and lower South.

Troubleshooting

Age often causes these shrubs to thin out at the base. Recapture their fullness by cutting the plants back to a foot tall and letting them grow again. Constant pruning ruins their rounded form.

AT A GLANCE
❖
WINTERGREEN BARBERRY
Berberis julianae

Features: spiny evergreen foliage, yellow flowers, blue fruit

Foliage: evergreen

Height: 6 to 8 feet

Width: 6 to 8 feet

Light: full sun to light shade

Soil: moist, well drained, slightly acid

Water: moderate

Range: Zones 5 to 8

Pests: none specific

Remarks: excellent for an impenetrable hedge

Crimson Pygmy Barberry

Crimson Pygmy barberry is actually just one selection of Japanese barberry *(Berberis thunbergii)* but it has become the most popular and widely planted selection of this tough group of plants because of its crimson foliage. It grows at a medium rate into a small mound, only 2 to 3 feet tall and slightly wider. Its manageable size makes it suitable for ground covers and perennial borders.

Crimson Pygmy barberry has small yellow flowers that open in midspring and are scarcely visible beneath the foliage. These pay bright dividends later, when the brilliant red fruit is revealed in fall.

In the Landscape

Use Crimson Pygmy barberry for a powerful, colorful accent in the landscape. The vivid color makes it a terrific specimen plant. Place it against a wall or beside an entry gate to signal direction. Think of this plant as punctuation; place it in front of more neutral backdrops, such as cleyera, or in a bed of a low, spreading ground cover.

Planting and Care

Plant Crimson Pygmy barberry in full sun; in partial sun, the foliage may revert to light green. This shrub prefers moist, well-drained, slightly acid soil. Once established, the plant is very drought tolerant; on the other hand, it does not like soggy soil. Crimson Pygmy and other Japanese barberries tolerate urban conditions very well.

Different Selections

There are many named selections of Japanese barberry that have reddish foliage color. Aurea has vivid yellow leaves that make a striking contrast with Crimson Pygmy barberry. Kobold resembles boxwood, with rich green foliage. Rosy Glow has near-pink new growth.

Troubleshooting

Crimson Pygmy barberry is rarely bothered by pests, except in the sandy soils of the lower South where root knot nematodes may limit its growth. See page 125 for more about this pest.

Crimson Pygmy barberry is striking between the yellow of patrinia and the deep green of juniper.

AT A GLANCE
❖
CRIMSON PYGMY BARBERRY
Berberis thunbergii var. *atropurpureum* Crimson Pygmy

Features: rich crimson foliage, fine texture
Foliage: deciduous
Height: 2 to 3 feet
Width: 3 to 4 feet
Light: full sun
Soil: moist, well drained
Water: moderate
Range: Zones 4 to 8
Pests: root knot nematodes
Remarks: tolerates urban conditions

Beautyberry

Beautyberry has stiff, upright branches that support the weight of the berries.

Beautyberry looks best in late summer and early fall, when its stems are dotted with an extraordinary array of magenta berries. Although this aptly named native shrub bears its major landscape attribute in one season, the berries are dazzling and offer a dramatic touch of color for the early weeks of fall.

The berry-laden branches of beautyberry are also prized for indoor arrangements. The shrub produces arching stems on a 4- to 8-foot plant that may be equally wide. These branches are used both for their strong line and deep color in fall decor.

The foliage of this sprawling shrub is dull green and coarse. The 4- to 6-inch-long leaves radiate around the stems; the arrangement of the leaves and the stiff branches reinforce the unrefined appearance of the shrub.

Clusters of pink flowers encircle the stems in midsummer and are noticeable but not showy. The berries appear before the leaves turn yellow in fall; after the leaves drop, the clusters of berries drape the shrub's twiggy form.

In the Landscape

Beautyberry is a challenge for gardeners—it is large and sprawling yet offers an unsurpassed, one-of-a kind show. Your best bet is to use it in naturalistic landscape plantings. Drift several beneath the open shade of large canopy trees in a natural area.

Place beautyberry in front of a backdrop, such as a fence, a wall, or other evergreens; this design trick shows off the vivid fruit when beautyberry loses its leaves early in the season. You may also plant low-growing evergreen shrubs around beautyberry. It is an excellent understory shrub to plant on large properties beneath tall pines; the trunks of the pines provide a handsome contrast to beautyberry's wild irregularity.

Planting and Care

To produce a good show of berries, beautyberry needs full sun or only light shade. In heavy shade it will not bear as much fruit as it will in sun. Choose a spot with moist but well-drained, slightly acid soil. Once established, this tough native plant can withstand both wet soil and prolonged periods of drought.

Species and Selections

Purple beautyberry is a different species, *Callicarpa dichotoma*, that is not native and grows just 2 to 4 feet high and slightly wider; it has long, slender branches that arch and touch the ground at their tips. The medium green foliage is arranged along the stem in one plane, giving the plant a more polished look. The berry show is outstanding. Purple beautyberry is a good choice for more formal gardens, as it is more refined and less sprawling than the native species.

Lactea, a white-fruited selection of beautyberry, is also available. Although the fruit is not as striking as the magenta berries of the species, its color is less likely to clash with other plants.

Lactea is a selection with white berries.

Beautyberry sprawls in a free-form arching mound that will quickly grow 4 to 8 feet high and equally wide.

Boxwood

Common boxwoods can stylishly guide visitors to the front door.

Boxwoods are among the most respected of landscape plants, having become an indispensable element in formal plantings and a standard of dignity and refinement in the garden. There is a mystique about boxwoods; they evoke formality regardless of surrounding plants. This evocative power is due in part to their perfect form, which makes a bold statement in the landscape, and to garden tradition. Long in cultivation, boxwoods reigned supreme in Europe before appearing in the Colonial gardens of America.

Another part of the appeal of boxwoods is their immutability. The plants rarely change, except to grow larger through the decades. The individual leaves are small and narrow, covering the plant thickly in a deep, evergreen layer of foliage. There is a softness about the leaves when you brush up against them, especially in early spring when the new growth surges bright, light green across the plant. Because the foliage is dense and the color remains constant, this shrub practically defines evergreen. Indeed, when you align several boxwoods within your garden, you create a visually captivating planting. Visitors will often remember the boxwoods in a garden and little else.

In the Landscape

A cluster of two or three common boxwoods flanking an entry is often the local definition of landscaping. This simple foundation treatment can be quite elegant, particularly if the architecture of the house is traditional or drawn from Colonial styles.

Edging boxwoods separate the lawn from the flower beds while reinforcing the walkway. They will eventually grow together to create a continuous edging.

While boxwoods perform formal design functions, such as framing a bench or an entry, these shrubs are not strictly rigid and formal. The tapering, upright, oval form of common boxwood makes it a handsome evergreen, as does the lumpy, rounded form of edging boxwood. Place a single specimen of each at the end of a perennial planting to serve as visual anchors for the season's color.

You may also use boxwood as an evergreen backdrop for a drift of spring bulbs or for a contrast of texture with coarse-leafed plants, such as peonies or iris. Planted at the edge of a lawn or garden, boxwoods may direct traffic around a bed, or you may position them beside walkways to enjoy the bright green new growth.

Boxwoods are one of few shrubs that look natural as a formal, sheared hedge; the tiny leaves accept shaping and do not brown along the cut edges. Shear them in December and use the cuttings for wreaths and centerpieces for the holidays.

You may use boxwoods with shrubs of different foliage texture, such as andromeda or cleyera. Coarse-textured ground covers, such as English ivy, are a wonderful underplanting for boxwoods.

There are few plants better suited to the framing of formal planting beds than slow-growing edging boxwood.

Planting and Care

Because you are likely to use boxwoods in a conspicuous location, give them the best possible care. They will grow in full sun to partial shade. In the southern portion of its range, plant boxwood under the high canopy of tall trees or where there is some protection from late afternoon sun and heat. Avoid direct summer sunlight, which can wither the foliage. This is not as critical from Virginia northward, however. Japanese boxwood *(Buxus microphylla* var. *japonica)* tolerates more sun than most types and does well in the deep South.

Where winter nights are very cold, shield boxwoods from morning sun; otherwise, the foliage may scald and turn reddish bronze. Although unsightly, the bronzing disappears when new growth resumes in spring. Unfortunately, a severe cold snap may kill the foliage, turning the ends of the twigs brittle and brown.

Boxwoods have shallow roots and prefer loose, well-drained soil that is rich in organic matter. Good drainage is essential; too much moisture increases the susceptibility to root rot. Boxwood does not like alkaline soil; a neutral or slightly acid soil is best.

When using boxwoods as a background for a flower bed, protect them from damage by not digging right up to the base of the plants. Keep the ground beneath boxwoods well mulched.

In time, these common boxwoods will create a niche for this bench.

Common boxwood creates a narrow entry garden for this home.

Troubleshooting

Boxwoods are bothered by four major pests, although maintaining a healthy plant greatly reduces the potential for problems. Leaf miners are the larvae of a fly that tunnels through the leaf tissue and disfigures the foliage. A plant can generally live with the damage unless more than half of its leaves are injured and the plant is weakened.

Psyllids feed on the tips of the branches, causing the new leaves to curl and look deformed. The tiny pest is easily recognized by a cottonlike covering on its body. Spider mites and root knot nematodes are also damaging. See page 125 for more about these pests.

Lower leaves and stems may be damaged by animal urine, which causes the foliage to turn brown and die.

Common Boxwood

Common boxwood grows into a rounded form. Because it grows at a moderate rate, the height of common boxwood is often underestimated; over several years, this long-lived shrub can reach a surprising height and spread of 15 feet. The foliage is deep, dark green on top and slightly lighter green on the underside. The shrub's large mature size makes it suitable for screening or hedge planting. It can be used as a foundation plant for a very large home.

Different Selections

Edging boxwood (*Buxus sempervirens* Suffruticosa) was one of the first plants introduced to the American colonies from Europe, an origin that led to its other common name, dwarf English boxwood. Edging boxwood is a slow-growing, popular selection of common boxwood. It creeps to a height of 3 to 4 feet and a spread of equal size but takes decades to do so. A very old single plant may be as much as 6 feet tall and just as wide. The foliage is rounded at the tips and lighter green than common boxwood. The plant becomes mounded, almost billowing in form, and is lumpy, not smoothly tapered. The foliage is very soft and pungent. While it is excellent for edging perennial beds or dividing schemes of color in parterre gardens, this shrub develops its most beautiful form when left unpruned.

Japanese Boxwood

Japanese boxwood is the best boxwood for the lower South, where humidity, heat, and sometimes alkaline soil do not allow common boxwood to grow. Although its form is looser and more open than edging boxwood, Japanese boxwood still brings a finely textured flair to the garden. The plant does not grow rapidly but does grow more quickly than common boxwood. It reaches a maximum height of about 4 feet with a similar spread; compact forms may only grow a foot tall. The leaves are slightly more rounded than those of edging boxwood and are deep green in color, though they turn yellowish brown in winter. The undersides of the upper leaves tend to be visible, a telltale sign for identification.

Japanese boxwood is a tough, durable plant, growing as far north as Tennessee and central North Carolina, but its strength is the fact that it is the best boxwood for the lower and coastal South. Wintergreen is an exceptionally cold-hardy selection that grows in the Midwest and is also popular in the hot, humid coastal South; its foliage turns bronze in winter.

Japanese boxwood is less susceptible to pests than common boxwood. However, root rot is a serious problem in soggy soil, so be sure the soil drains well where you plant it.

Korean Boxwood

Korean boxwood, sometimes called littleleaf boxwood, is considered the hardiest of all boxwoods, surviving in the cold of the Midwest and New England as far north as Zone 4. Surprisingly, this is also one of the most heat-tolerant boxwoods, extending its range to Texas and Florida. Korean boxwood is a dense, slow-growing plant with extremely small, finely textured foliage and an open, loosely rounded form. This tough evergreen is more similar to edging boxwood than any other boxwood. It also stays small, rarely growing taller than 2 feet. Tide Hill is a selection that stays low (less than 2 feet tall) but can spread to twice its height.

In the heat of the South, Japanese boxwood takes the place of edging boxwood.

AT A GLANCE
❖
JAPANESE BOXWOOD
Buxus microphylla var. *japonica*

Features: deep color; small, rounded leaves
Foliage: evergreen
Height: 1 to 4 feet
Width: 3 to 4 feet
Light: partial sun
Soil: rich, well drained
Water: moderate
Range: Zones 6 to 9
Pests: leaf miners, psyllids, spider mites, root knot nematodes
Remarks: more heat tolerant than common boxwood

Camellia

This common camellia, Pink Perfection, has a formal double flower.

Camellias rival azaleas in popularity in the South. These long-lived plants often last through several generations of gardeners, who cherish them for their dark, glossy, evergreen foliage and brightly colored flowers in late winter and early spring. Although they are originally from Japan, they have become a traditional Southern flower. With time, these handsome evergreens can reach 10 to 15 feet in height and 6 to 10 feet in width.

Planting and Care

Camellias are good understory plants that require protection from the searing midday and early afternoon sun. (Sasanqua camellias are more tolerant of sun than common camellias.) Plant common camellias in shade in rich, well-drained, slightly acid soil. In poorly drained areas, camellia is susceptible to root rot. Severe freezes can knock a camellia back to the ground or completely kill it, so it may need protection from extreme cold. Winter winds may also burn the foliage; help prevent this by spraying with an antidesiccant.

Troubleshooting

You may see the margins of the leaves turn yellow while the veins remain green. This condition is called chlorosis and usually indicates a lack of iron. Chlorosis is worst in areas where the soil or water is alkaline. You can correct this condition by applying iron chelate to the soil around the plant. Also, be sure to use an acid-forming azalea/camellia food each time you fertilize in spring.

Tea scale is a tiny, white, hard scale that attaches to the stems and the underside of the leaves; infested leaves turn yellow and drop. A severe infestation will eventually kill the shrub. The best way to combat tea scale is to spray the plants each winter and spring with a dormant oil, which coats the eggs, keeping the young from hatching. See page 125 for more about scales.

Common Camellia

Common camellia is the best known of all camellias, producing large, waxy blooms in winter and spring in Zones 7 to 9, where winters are mild. These are classic Southern plants but are also popular along the West Coast. Selections bloom from November through March or April.

AT A GLANCE
❖
COMMON CAMELLIA
Camellia japonica

Features: glossy, evergreen foliage; exquisite flowers

Foliage: evergreen

Height: 10 to 15 feet

Width: 6 to 10 feet

Light: partial shade

Soil: moist, well drained, slightly acid

Water: moderate

Range: Zones 7 to 9

Pests: tea scale

Remarks: provides brilliant color in winter

In the Landscape

The upright, pyramidal form of common camellia looks best when planted near structures, such as an entrance gate or a gazebo, or in a formal setting, such as a Colonial garden. Larger plants may frame a seating area or serve as a dense evergreen screen. Common camellia also works well in foundation plantings at the slightly shaded corner of a residence or as a focal point in a side yard.

Pair it with a contrasting plant, such as edging boxwood or oakleaf hydrangea; the shrub will also blend well with Burford holly, cleyera, or aucuba in an informal screen in the shade. You may use common camellia along a woodland path to be the evergreen anchors for smaller plantings in the border. In the lower and coastal South, you may use camellias as single specimens; remove the lower limbs of old plants to train them into a treelike form.

Different Selections

There are dozens of camellia hybrids. You can choose one based on the time of bloom, ultimate size, habit of growth, and cold hardiness. Flowers may be single or very full; their colors range from white to multicolored and include various shades of red, rose, lavender, and pink.

While most selections are reliably hardy in Zones 8 and 9, not all are hardy in Zone 7; always check with a local source for hybrids proven in your area. Winter's Charm, Ice Follies, and Polar Ice are three of several selections that endure temperatures of at least 10 degrees below zero, stretching the range to Zone 6.

A large common camellia frames the corner of this one-story house.

Camellia blooms boast a porcelain-like perfection.

Blooming times vary with the individual hybrids. Most selections bloom in February or March, but cold winters may delay bloom until April and a sudden freeze will reduce the most exquisite flowers to brown, wilted mush. By choosing selections that bloom at different times (from November to March or April) you can enjoy camellias for five or six months of the year.

Sasanqua Camellia

Sasanqua camellia blooms much earlier than common camellia, usually before Thanksgiving. Although it is a handsome shrub even when it is not in bloom, it is the unexpected fall flowers that are sasanqua's greatest attraction.

This shrub is less rigid and pyramidal than common camellia. Instead, it has a looser, more rounded form that gives it a casual appearance. The more open growth habit also makes it more adaptable to a wider range of garden uses, including espalier.

Sasanqua grows slowly to 6 to 10 feet high. The glossy evergreen leaves are smaller than those of common camellia; they are usually about 2 inches long with slightly serrated edges. The flowers are also smaller, 1 to 3 inches in diameter, which adds to this shrub's more delicate appearance.

When pruned as an espalier, sasanqua camellia elegantly softens the architecture.

AT A GLANCE
❖
SASANQUA CAMELLIA
Camellia sasanqua

Features: glossy, evergreen foliage; profuse fall flowers

Foliage: evergreen

Height: 6 to 10 feet, sometimes 15 feet

Width: 4 to 8 feet

Light: partial shade

Soil: moist, well drained, slightly acid

Water: moderate

Range: Zones 7 to 9

Pests: tea scale

Remarks: fabulous fall blooms

In the Landscape

Sasanqua camellias prefer shade but are tolerant of sun, permitting you to integrate them into shrub borders with great flexibility. They may provide an evergreen backdrop for bright but short-lived blooms, such as kerria.

Sasanquas form a dependable screen or hedge. The evergreen foliage also makes them excellent backdrop shrubs for a perennial planting or for bolstering a layered planting of low-growing shrubs, such as Gumpo azaleas.

Because its handsome foliage remains dark green year-round, sasanqua works well as an entry feature at the gates of a driveway or in an informal grouping at the corner of a residence. You will often see sasanquas drifted under the shade of high pine trees. It is a handsome understory addition to existing pines, where it can be the evergreen backdrop for ferns, bulbs, annuals, and perennials. Older plants, which may have reached a mature height of about 15 feet, can be trained as treelike shrubs by removing the lower limbs.

Sasanquas also make beautiful espaliers. This is an ambitious use that requires regular (and careful) pruning, but the effect is usually worth the effort.

Different Selections

Like common camellias, sasanqua camellias are limited to Zones 8 to 9, although many survive in Zone 7 until a periodic hard freeze kills the plant. Unless you live where sasanqua hardiness is guaranteed, check locally for those selections proven in your area. Popular selections include Shishi-Gashira, with bright pink blooms, and Bonanza, a low-growing, spreading type that bears red blooms and may be used as a tall ground cover.

Sasanqua camellia is a handsome shrub for marking an entry.

Cleyera

The leaves of cleyera are instantly distinguished by their high gloss and whorled arrangement on the stem.

Cleyera is known for its glossy, evergreen foliage that looks as if it has been polished. This is a handsome, sturdy shrub of medium height that is useful for screening. Often called Japanese cleyera, this versatile shrub is native to Asia. It grows slowly to an upright, rounded form that is 8 to 10 feet tall and half as wide. Its glossy, 2-inch leaves feel almost rubbery; they are clustered in whorls at the tips of the layered branches.

Although it is evergreen, cleyera shows remarkable color change from spring until winter. Spring's fresh new growth is brilliant copper and slowly darkens to bronze, before turning a deep blackish green in summer. In winter, cleyera takes on a rich burgundy blush which may, during prolonged periods of cold, become a vivid wine red.

Creamy white flowers, often hidden by the foliage, open in late spring, exuding a delicate sweet scent. The blooms ripen in autumn to become clusters of orange-red berries that remain throughout the winter.

The fruit ripens in fall and splits open to reveal red seeds inside.

In the Landscape

An architectural feature, such as a fence, a wall, or an outbuilding, is an excellent backdrop to the open form and whorled foliage of cleyera. At the same time, the structures are partially screened by the handsome evergreen foliage. In small courtyards, cleyera is a good choice to fill a corner of the garden. Use it at the corner of a foundation planting or at places of prominence, such as entry gates.

Cleyera can be drifted casually beneath a high shade canopy to create an informal screen. The shrub may also be used as an accent in plantings of other shrubs with contrasting color, such as Wheeler's Dwarf pittosporum or Crimson Pygmy barberry. It works well with a fine-textured ground cover, such as mondo grass.

Planting and Care

Cleyera needs protection from winter winds in the colder regions of Zone 7, the northern limit of its hardiness, but even with protection it may die back. It does best in slight shade, although it will grow

---

AT A GLANCE
❖
CLEYERA
Ternstroemia gymnanthera

Features: elegant, glossy foliage

Foliage: evergreen

Height: 8 to 10 feet

Width: 5 to 6 feet

Light: partial shade to full sun

Soil: moist, well drained

Water: moderate

Range: Zones 7 to 9

Pests: none specific

Remarks: a handsome plant for accent use

Cleyera is a very useful upright evergreen that is neither too small or too big, working well in many niches of a garden.

well in full sun once established. Cleyera will tolerate a variety of soils, but good drainage is a must. Avoid planting in very heavy clay or in poorly drained locations.

Different Selections

There are few named selections of this shrub. Variegata has variegated foliage; its dark green leaves are marbled with gray and have creamy edges that blush pink in cold weather. This selection, however, is not as vigorous. You will often see cleyera listed by another scientific name, *Cleyera japonica*. However, most plants sold under this name are actually *Ternstroemia gymnanthera*. The shrubs are almost identical except that *Cleyera japonica* has smaller leaves.

Cotoneaster

Rockspray cotoneaster grows low to the ground and may be laden with berries in fall.

Cotoneasters are a group known for their arching forms, prolific spring flowers, and bright red fruit that appears in early fall. They range from tall, almost hedgelike plants to prostrate and miniature leafed.

Spring foliage emerges bright green. In late spring, tiny red, white, or slightly pink blooms cover the plant. Red berries become visible by late summer and have a landscape impact through winter or until eaten by birds.

In the Landscape

There are two landscape uses for which cotoneasters seem especially well suited: as a carpeting ground cover in an informal, naturalistic setting or as a cover on a sloping portion of a lot.

These shrubs are nearly without equal when positioned to drape over a wall or to mound and spread about rock outcroppings. They are also helpful for erosion control because the branches of some types root where they touch the earth. Due to their twiggy habit and beautiful fruit, many cotoneasters are also prized as espaliers.

Single specimens of the low-growing cotoneasters may be used as colorful accents, while the taller species and selections, such as willowleaf cotoneaster, are useful in border plantings.

Planting and Care

Cotoneasters prefer well-drained, loose, fertile soil with adequate moisture; a soggy site is certain to kill them. Once established, they withstand dry, poor soil and the neglect common to commercial plantings. These shrubs will grow in acid or alkaline soil. While the plants are fullest in sunny locations, they also tolerate light shade.

Species and Selections

Bearberry cotoneaster (*Cotoneaster dammeri*) is used as an evergreen ground cover for quick and dependable coverage. The plant will grow less than 3 feet tall but will spread as much as 6 feet across in a dense, twiggy tangle; the stems root where they touch the ground. Lowfast is extremely hardy and stays true to its name at about 1 foot in height. Skogsholmen is also extremely low growing and spreads as much as 2 feet a year.

Creeping cotoneaster (*Cotoneaster adpressus* var. *praecox*) has stems that root where they touch the soil, making it a good choice for planting on banks or other areas where you want to prevent erosion.

AT A GLANCE

❖

COTONEASTER
Cotoneaster species

Features: mounding or spreading growth, prolific red fruit

Foliage: deciduous and evergreen

Height: 1 to 10 feet

Width: 3 to 6 feet

Light: full sun to light shade

Soil: moist, well drained

Water: moderate

Range: Zones 4 to 8

Pests: cotoneaster webworm, lacebugs, spider mites, fire blight

Remarks: dependable shrubs with a variety of uses

Rockspray cotoneaster *(Cotoneaster horizontalis)*, a deciduous plant, stays low to the ground (about 3 feet in height). The branches tend to form layers that give the plant an interesting, architectural look.

Willowleaf cotoneaster *(Cotoneaster salicifolius)* is much taller than other cotoneasters, often reaching 10 feet in height in an upright, fountainous form. Its evergreen, 3½-inch narrow leaves turn burgundy in winter. The clusters of large berries are also striking. It is popular for espalier or in a shrub border. Repens is a prostrate selection that is only 2 feet tall but may spread 6 feet or more.

Troubleshooting

Cotoneaster webworm is a yellow caterpillar that makes webs at the base of the branches. These pests also feed on green leaf tissue, often leaving only the veins. Turn to page 124 for more about caterpillars.

Lacebugs and spider mites will often attack this shrub. Occasionally plants may be infected by fire blight, a bacterial disease that causes the leaves and twigs to die back. Turn to pages 124-125 to read more about lacebugs, spider mites, and fire blight.

Willowleaf cotoneaster makes an excellent espalier.

Elaeagnus

The tiny flowers of elaeagnus belie the power of their fragrance in the fall.

Fruitland elaeagnus is a selection of thorny elaeagnus that sprawls to become a large, evergreen thicket. It is durable enough to survive in the medians of interstate highways and the salt-spray zone of beachfront plantings along the coast. Wherever it is planted, it will quickly grow to 8 to 10 feet high and 15 feet wide. While not a shrub for small lots, fruitland elaeagnus is a good choice for large places where you want an evergreen to inexpensively cover a large, sunny, exposed area, such as the property line between large lots.

Softening the character of fruitland elaeagnus is the fragrance of countless inconspicuous fall flowers. These small, bell-shaped ornaments remain nearly hidden by the foliage but announce the shrub with a fragrance as powerful as that of gardenia. The scent alone rewards finding a place in the garden for this tough evergreen. The flowers are followed by a small, brownish-silver fruit that appears in late fall and early winter; birds like both the berries and the dense foliage, which is good for safe nesting.

Fruitland elaeagnus has an upright, fountainlike growth habit and grows by thrusting tentacle-like shoots skyward. Gardeners who prefer neat, tidy shrubs find this growth characteristic an annoyance. However, these long shoots are prized for indoor flower and foliage arrangements. The leaves are about 2 inches long and 1 to 1½ inches wide. They have a bronze cast and silvery undersides that give a metallic shimmer in the breeze and can do the same in an indoor arrangement.

In the Landscape

Elaeagnus makes a dense, attractive screen or privacy hedge even when spaced 10 feet apart. Often this shrub is planted without enough room for it to sprawl and is subject to unfortunate pruning. The shrub is valued for its natural arching character, so plant it along a property line where ample space is available. Allow at least 8 feet between this shrub and other plantings or structures.

A single plant can be used effectively at the edge of a wooded area as a year-round accent. Place it where the scent of the flowers may waft through the remainder of the garden. Consider it also for steeply sloping banks and other difficult landscape situations in which vigorous evergreen growth and size are useful. Keep it at the top of the list for plantings on property that is subject to salt spray.

Planting and Care

Plant elaeagnus either in full sun or partial shade in practically any soil. Its growth is slowed when it is planted in heavily compacted soil or high clay subsoils, however. It is tolerant of heat and thrives in poor, sandy soil.

Elaeagnus needs little care once established, provided you have allowed enough room to let it grow without pruning.

Species and Selections

Aurea has leaves edged with bright yellow and Maculata has large leaves marked with a deep yellow blotch in the center of the leaf. Silverberry, *Elaeagnus* x *ebbengi,* is a thornless hybrid that includes the selection Gilt Edge, whose leaves are banded with golden yellow.

Troubleshooting

Elaeagnus is a trouble-free plant. Spider mites may infest it in dry weather, but it generally outgrows the damage without your intervention. Turn to page 125 to read more about spider mites.

These young, variegated elaeagnus add unexpected brightness to the landscape.

Euonymus

Corky "wings" along the twigs give the shrub one of its names, winged euonymus. This feature is most visible after the leaves drop.

The most striking shrub of the fall landscape is winged euonymus, also called burning bush. This shrub is vivid from several blocks away. The color change comes early, often two weeks before most other deciduous plants, so the fiery-red winged euonymus is contrasted against a green backdrop. It often holds its hue for as long as a month. The fall show is a surprise because the plant is rather unassuming in summer, despite its vase-shaped form and finely textured foliage.

There are two forms of winged euonymus: large and compact. The large form, *Euonymus alata,* grows to become a wide, rounded shrub at least 15 feet tall and equally wide.

The compact form, *Euonymus alata* compacta, is actually more widely used than the larger plant. When the foliage drops, both produce clusters of tiny fruiting capsules that split when the seeds are mature, revealing the orange fruit inside. The seed capsules stay on the branches long after the seeds fall, adding another ornamental aspect to the branching of this large shrub.

The leafless months showcase the almost perfectly symmetrical growth habit of this shrub. As it matures, the plant assumes a vase or fountain shape, with branches arching to almost touch the ground. Long, corky growths project along its branches to give the leafless shrub a sculptural look. However, the wings are less prominent on the compact form.

AT A GLANCE

❖

WINGED EUONYMUS
Euonymus alata

Features: brilliant fall foliage
Foliage: deciduous
Height: 6 to 20 feet
Width: 10 to 15 feet
Light: full sun
Soil: moist, well drained
Water: moderate
Range: Zones 3 to 8
Pests: none specific
Remarks: needs a lot of room

The native type of winged euonymus can grow tall enough to form a small tree.

In the Landscape

The orderly vase-shaped form, rounded outline, and neutral green of the growing season foliage make winged euonymus a splendid choice for informal hedges, mass plantings, or edging accents of a natural area. But beware—it needs room to reach its mature height and spread.

The fall color is so bright that it will be noticed in any location, but a dark evergreen backdrop, such as Norway spruce, makes the color appear even more intense. A neutral backdrop, such as a weathered redwood or pine fence, also emphasizes the color. Evergreen understory plantings also provide a contrasting color to the fall show.

The vivid color and intricate branching make this plant lovely when viewed from beneath. Older shrubs can be pruned from their fully branched form into a treelike shrub by removing the lower branches. Most are large enough to shelter a garden bench and allow you to pass beneath and will blend into the understory trees and shrubs at a woodland edge.

Given the needed room, winged euonymus will grow into a large, maintenance-free hedge.

Planting and Care

Winged euonymus will grow in nearly any well-drained soil. It does not like wet sites; however, it does require a location where the soil stays moist during periods of drought or it will need to be watered regularly.

Plant winged euonymus in either full sun or light shade. Full sun yields much better fall color.

Different Selections

The large winged euonymus is less common and is sold simply as the species, with few named selections available. Compacta, a dwarf form, is more widely available than the parent. However, do not be misled by the name; it is not a small plant, growing to 10 feet tall and equally wide. Allow at least 6 feet between plants in hedge plantings or from a path, a driveway, or a wall. Rudy Haag is a bit smaller, reaching 5 to 6 feet in height.

The orderly foliage of dwarf winged euonymus is a nicely layered, steady green during the growing season.

Fatsia

The large, lobed leaves of fatsia give the plant a tropical look.

Fatsia fills a niche by providing evergreen foliage in deep shade, such as under a high deck or other places where the sun never shines. The deeply lobed leaves are often a foot wide and are a deep, lustrous green. The leaf shape and the plant's rounded, open growth habit bring a tropical flair to the shadowy parts of your garden.

Fatsia grows at a moderate to rapid rate to 6 to 8 feet in both height and spread. In the middle South, even in protected locations, freezes will kill the top to the ground, but it comes back from the roots like a perennial.

This shrub also rewards you with a peculiar flower show—stalks of rounded clusters of white flowers—that appear in October and November. The flowers are followed by fleshy black berries.

In the Landscape

Fatsia is so coarsely textured that anywhere you put it, it will draw your eye. Place it in a shady planter adjacent to an entry or mass it along the edge of a terrace to create the effect of a tropical retreat. For dramatic contrast, try planting a single specimen in a bed of finely textured ground cover, such as mondo grass or periwinkle, or combine the plant with English ivy, holly fern, or other plants that prefer deep shade.

Planting and Care

Place fatsia in the shade, as direct sun will cause the plant to brown. It can tolerate a certain amount of filtered light, but too much sun will burn the leaves; prolonged exposure will eventually kill the plant. It

AT A GLANCE

❖

FATSIA
Fatsia japonica

Features: bold, coarse foliage in deep shade

Foliage: evergreen

Height: 6 to 8 feet

Width: usually 6 to 8 feet

Light: shade to partial shade

Soil: moist, well drained, rich

Water: moderate

Range: Zones 8 to 10

Pests: none specific

Remarks: has a tropical look

will grow as far north as Atlanta but must be sheltered. Winter temperatures lower than 10 degrees will cause it to die back, but it will resprout in spring, especially if protected with a layer of mulch.

Fatsia prefers well-drained, acid soil that is rich in organic matter. It can tolerate a short period of drought or an occasional flooding but will struggle if these conditions persist.

If possible, select a plant with several stems since this will produce a more compact, bushy plant.

Different Selections

There are several selections of fatsia. Aurea has golden variegated leaves. Moseri is a more compact form with larger leaves. Variegata has a white coloration across the leaf, primarily at the lobe's end.

Moseri has been crossed with English ivy *(Hedera helix)* to produce x *Fatshedera lizei,* an unusual hybrid. This is a climbing plant that resembles fatsia in leaf shape and plant texture. It prefers deep shade and may be trained to a wall or a trellis.

Fatsia attracts attention because of its unusual foliage and bold texture.

Flowering Quince

Nivalis is a pure white selection of flowering quince.

An old-fashioned, one-season wonder, this shrub is a marvelous tangle of spines, twigs, and blossoms. Perhaps the champion early-blooming shrub, it introduces spring with both brilliant and soft pastel colors as early as February in the warmest parts of its range. Two or three successive warm winter days will coax flowering quince out of hibernation and into bloom.

The fruit of flowering quince appears in summer and is occasionally harvested to make jelly.

Flowering quince grows quickly into a large, upright, rounded plant, easily reaching 6 to 10 feet tall and equally wide. It is extraordinarily hardy and will survive from Zone 4 to Zone 9.

Most gardeners plant quince for its sculptural flowers alone. They are simple and delicate, borne singly and in clusters along the spiny, gray-brown branches. The flowers are extremely resistant to freezing weather and emerge almost two weeks before the foliage. Blooms may persist for almost a month in sporadic displays. Colors range from pure white to deep orange red.

Following bloom, quince spends the late spring and early summer without notice, clad in deep green foliage. It loses some leaves in July and August, revealing yellow fruit that is used for making preserves. The remaining leaves turn lemon yellow in the fall.

In the Landscape

The upright, rounded shape of flowering quince can be used in a shrub border in conjunction with other plants; the shrub does not have enough appeal throughout the year to be successful in a massed planting. It does look very good when isolated at a wooded edge, where it may flower and then fade from importance.

Lesser flowering quince, a smaller species, has more garden utility because of its manageable size. It makes a fine deciduous ground cover in front of an evergreen hedge or screen planting or as an accent shrub along a split-rail fence or a brick wall. It mixes well with the dark, evergreen needles of Japanese black pine.

AT A GLANCE
❖
FLOWERING QUINCE
Chaenomeles hybrids

Features: splendid early
    flowers
Foliage: deciduous
Height: 6 to 10 feet
Width: 6 to 10 feet
Light: full sun to light shade
Soil: well drained
Water: moderate
Range: Zones 4 to 9
Pests: none specific
Remarks: provides exquisite
    flowers in the garden

Planting and Care

Flowering quince grows best in full sun or partial shade; sunny locations produce more flowers. It will tolerate the reflected heat on the south and west sides of a building and will survive prolonged drought. It needs well-drained soil but will grow in sandy or clay soil if provided good drainage.

Give quince plenty of room or plan to prune it. Late winter or early spring is the best time to prune so that you can take the branches inside where warmth will force the buds to open. Branch removal will encourage new growth for the following season.

Different Selections

There are many selections of flowering quince, some of which are the result of crosses with lesser flowering quince. The best time to choose quince is when the plant is in bloom so you can be sure of the color of its flowers. Cameo has double, apricot-colored blooms and a compact spreading habit, about 3 feet tall and 5 feet wide. Texas Scarlet has vivid red flowers and reaches about the same size as Cameo. Moned is an 8-foot-tall plant with very large flowers. Nivalis is also large and bears white flowers. Apple Blossom is upright with light pink flowers.

Flowering quince arrives with the earliest daffodils to make a spring greeting.

Troubleshooting

Scab is a fungus that often defoliates quince by the end of summer, but it will not reduce bloom the next year.

Pink and white quince frame a split-rail fence, showing off when in bloom and then receding for the rest of the year.

Forsythia

A forsythia in full bloom is a sure sign that spring has arrived.

Few plants chase winter with the vigor and enthusiasm of forsythia. Just when you think the gray skies will last forever, this deciduous, old-fashioned favorite bursts into a fountain of yellow blooms.

There are many hybrids of forsythia but all have a gently arching form and a spreading growth habit. Young plants will not have this graceful curve during their rapid surge to maturity; they will be stiff until they reach their full height and spread. The shoots of an immature plant will tend to grow straight up, giving the plant a spiky effect, but as it ages, the branches lengthen and droop, developing the characteristic mounding, informal habit.

Larger forsythia have 3- to 5-inch rich green leaves during the growing season that turn yellow green and sometimes maroon in fall. Even in winter, the dense twig structure is thick enough to be a privacy screen. Smaller hybrids have smaller leaves and compact stems.

In the Landscape

Forsythia is flamboyant in spring and nearly inconspicuous during the rest of the year. Whether you plant several as an informal hedge or use a solitary specimen to accent a border, this shrub is perfect for distant garden locations beyond a kitchen or bedroom window, where the blooming branches are silhouetted against the darker backdrop of natural woods, a wall, or a fence.

Forsythia grows large enough and remains visually dense enough to serve as a privacy planting. On larger properties, it works well in combination with evergreen shrubs, such as wax myrtle or ligustrum. Pair it with loblolly pines or Leyland cypress to create a free-flowing border.

Avoid planting forsythia in foundations or in borders less than 8 feet wide—it will quickly outgrow such locations. Give it plenty of room; this plant's size is often underestimated. Pruning is not recommended as the shrub's natural form is one of its greatest assets.

Planting and Care

Forsythia needs full sun for best bloom. It grows in almost any type of soil and, once established, requires little attention at all. Although tolerant of drought, forsythia does need occasional watering.

Every three or four years, remove the oldest canes to permit younger, more vigorous shoots to come up from the base. Do this immediately after the shrub blooms, in early spring, so that the new growth will develop flower buds for the following spring.

In full bloom, an unpruned forsythia is truly a fountain of color.

Different Selections

There are many selections of forsythia that vary in both the size of the bloom and the size and form of the shrub. Arnold Dwarf has greenish-yellow flowers that are sparse. It stays lower than most, growing only 3 to 4 feet tall, and is a good choice for a ground cover for large sunny expanses; it roots where the stems touch the ground, so give it plenty of room to spread. Beatrix Farrand is a large, upright shrub with a dense habit of growth and golden yellow flowers that are 1½ to 2 inches across. Karl Sax offers deep yellow flowers held horizontally on the stems. Lynwood is a rather stiff, vertical plant with brassy yellow flowers. Spectabilis is similar to Beatrix Farrand but has larger flowers that appear in greater profusion. Spring Glory is prized for its extremely large, soft yellow flowers.

Meadowlark is a hybrid forsythia that is quite cold hardy and is often used in the Midwest because its flower buds are not as likely to die when the temperature dips 10 to 20 degrees below zero. It grows about 9 feet high.

Gardenia

Some selections have large double flowers.

Although the glossy evergreen foliage of gardenia is beautiful, this shrub is primarily grown for one reason: the intoxicating fragrance of its blooms. A single shrub will perfume an entire garden, and the aroma of the cut flowers will fill your home. Be sure to plant a gardenia near your deck or patio.

Gardenia grows from 4 to 6 feet tall and equally wide. In late spring, it is covered with soft, silky white blooms. Plants often continue blooming on and off through summer. When properly maintained, the shrub is a dark green, handsome evergreen. The 2- to 4-inch-long, deeply ribbed leaves give the plant a medium texture. In areas where gardenia is not hardy, plant it in a large pot and bring it indoors during the winter.

In the Landscape

Gardenia has many landscape uses in addition to its fragrance. A grouping is a good evergreen background for shade or a single plant may be used in a shrub border or a foundation planting. Most gardenias grow in a rounded form that will stay full to the bottom and serve well as a short, unpruned hedge or screen. If you grow gardenias in a container, choose a pot at least 16 inches in diameter to provide enough soil volume and moisture for good growth.

Planting and Care

Gardenia is not a carefree shrub, but its fragrance is worth the extra effort. The plant needs moist, acid soil that is rich in organic matter. The leaves will develop chlorosis, turning yellow in soil that is not acid. Fertilize with an azalea/camellia food to provide the extra iron needed to keep the foliage deep green. Proper conditions are essential, as gardenia is more susceptible to insects when struggling.

Gardenia prefers partial shade, especially in the afternoon. However, if given enough water, it will also grow in full sun. Although only hardy through Zones 8 to 10, some gardenias will grow in protected locations through Zone 7. The shrub should provide several years of delightful blooms and foliage before being killed by cold winter weather.

Different Selections

While gardenia is rarely sold by any name other than gardenia, you should be aware that there are several available selections of the shrub. The selections vary slightly. Mystery and August Beauty both have large (4- to 5-inch) double white flowers; they grow to about 8 feet tall. Fortuniana has very large leaves and 4-inch full flowers. Veitchii is a smaller shrub, growing to about 4 feet tall; it also produces smaller flowers but is apt to bloom continuously through the summer and fall. First Love™ is a selection with extra-large double blooms that appear throughout the growing season.

Dwarf gardenia (*Gardenia jasminoides* 'Radicans') is a small, creeping gardenia with small leaves and small, fragrant blooms. Dwarf gardenia is popular as a ground cover for partial shade. When full grown, the plants are rarely over 2 feet tall but may be 3 to 4 feet wide. Dwarf gardenia is not quite as hardy as the large gardenia and will need winter protection during a severe freeze.

The alluring fragrance of gardenia blooms is reason enough to plant the shrub in your garden.

Troubleshooting

Gardenia is prone to many pests, but healthy plants growing in partial shade are less susceptible to attack and better able to recover. Look for aphids, scales, spider mites, and root knot nematodes. See pages 124–125 for more about these pests. Gardenias may also be bothered by thrips, whiteflies, and mealybugs. It is normal for gardenias to drop leaves in spring and early summer, so do not be alarmed. Even though they are evergreen, the old leaves do fall off as others replace them. You may also see leaves turn yellow between the veins, especially after flowering. This usually indicates that a plant needs iron, so be sure to fertilize with a product that contains extra iron or apply a solution of liquid iron according to directions on the product label.

Hawthorn

Indian hawthorn bears waxy blue berries in late summer.

AT A GLANCE
❖

INDIAN HAWTHORN
Raphiolepis indica

Features: handsome foliage, mounding habit, fragrant flowers

Foliage: evergreen

Height: 4 to 10 feet

Width: 4 to 10 feet

Light: full sun

Soil: moist, well drained

Water: moderate

Range: Zones 8 to 10

Pests: leaf spot

Remarks: durable, salt-tolerant evergreen for coastal settings

Indian hawthorn brings bright flowers atop lush evergreen foliage to the sunny spring landscape. Easy to grow, it is a durable choice in the lower South when you are searching for a neat shrub that requires little maintenance and tolerates heat, humidity, and salt spray.

The leaves are dark glossy green with a leathery look that seems to reflect sunshine. They have softly serrated edges and are slightly rounded at the tips.

Indian hawthorn's April blooms range in color from white to deep pink. They are fragrant, but the strength of their fragrance varies among selections. The flowers are followed in late summer by waxy blue berries.

In the Landscape

Low-growing selections combine well with other low-growing plants in a border or a foundation planting. In the lower South, Indian hawthorn is a popular shrub to plant near patios and swimming pools or other sun-drenched locations. Use Indian hawthorn to edge a border of tall shrubs, ranging from wax myrtle to pampas grass. One effective use is to drift the plants in an open lawn.

Taller species may serve as a background plant in flower borders or as an anchor shrub at the corner of a foundation planting. Both the small and large species are perfect for containers, as they are tolerant of hot, dry conditions and their roots do not suffer in restricted space.

The plant will survive the harsh conditions of coastal zones; it will adapt to sandy soil and is tolerant of salt spray.

Planting and Care

Once established, Indian hawthorn is drought tolerant. For best growth, plant in fertile, well-drained soil in full sun. Be sure to provide a steady, moderate amount of water.

Temperatures of 10 degrees or less will damage the plant. Protect it from extreme weather at the northern limits of its range.

Species and Selections

Indian hawthorn includes several selections, all of which vary slightly in flower color, leaf size, and height. Enchantress is a compact form that is 3 to 4 feet in height with rose pink flowers. Fascination, also compact, has pink-and-white flowers. Snow White is a dwarf spreading form with white flowers and lighter green foliage.

Yedda hawthorn *(Raphiolepis umbellata),* a related species, is sometimes called Indian hawthorn. However, this plant is much larger than Indian hawthorn and is often trained as a tree-form shrub.

There are several hybrids of these and other related species. Majestic Beauty is a hybrid that reaches 10 feet or more in height with 4-inch-long leaves and is often trained to tree form. It bears large clusters (6 inches in diameter) of fragrant pink blooms.

Troubleshooting

Leaf spot can disfigure or completely defoliate a plant, especially in shady locations where the foliage stays moist from dew many hours a day. You can avoid this disease by planting the shrub in a hot, sunny location. Some hybrids show better resistance to leaf spot.

The dense mounding habit of growth of Indian hawthorn makes it excellent for low plantings between a driveway and the street.

Holly

Burford holly is a self-fruiting selection that bears prolific berries each year.

Hollies are among the most varied landscape plants; they can be large or small, deciduous or evergreen, low mounding or high arching. Basically, there is a holly for every landscape situation.

Chinese Holly

While Chinese holly is famous for its evergreen, glossy foliage, it is equally infamous for the needle-sharp spines along the edges of its leaves. The leaves, which have a plastic texture, seem to be pulled and stretched at the spiny nodes.

The original Chinese holly is rarely available in garden centers, having been replaced by newer hybrids. Some of its better traits—hardiness, adaptability, shiny evergreen foliage—have survived in numerous popular selections. Two of these, Burford and Rotunda, are strong, attractive shrubs that thrive in hot, sunny places.

Different Selections in the Landscape

Burford holly (*Ilex cornuta* Burfordii) is a broadly rounded, coarse-textured, fast-growing selection that reaches a treelike height of 15 to 20 feet in less than 20 years. It has dark green, glossy, 1½- to 3-inch-long leaves that have a single spine at the end. It is best known for its large, orange-red berries that appear in fall.

Burford holly becomes a living wall. Place it along the property line as a large hedge. Give the shrub plenty of room and do not be tempted to shear it; the leaves turn brown along the edges when cut.

This holly is simply too large for foundation plantings unless it is trained as a tree to be used as an accent. If you have an overgrown Burford holly, you may rehabilitate it by removing the lower limbs to reveal the trunk; let the top grow into a small tree.

Dwarf Burford holly (*Ilex cornuta* Burfordii Nana) reaches 8 feet in height. Use it much as you would the standard Burford but where an 8-foot shrub is better suited than a 15- to 20-foot one.

Carissa holly is a low, mounding form used in masses, under windows, and as an anchor. It bears 2- to 3-inch dark green leaves with a single spine at the end. It does not produce berries.

Rotunda holly grows into a spiny thicket 3 to 4 feet tall and 6 to 8 feet wide. It survives hot, dry sites, including the reflected heat from pavement. The leaves have seven sharp spines so use Rotunda holly only in areas where you do not want any foot traffic. It does not produce berries.

AT A GLANCE

❖

CHINESE HOLLY
Ilex cornuta

Features: glossy foliage, terrific durability

Foliage: evergreen

Height: 3 to 20 feet

Width: 3 to 20 feet

Light: full sun

Soil: well drained

Water: low

Range: Zones 7 to 9

Pests: spider mites

Remarks: durable, dependable evergreens for full sun

Planting and Care

Chinese hollies will grow in clay or sand but need good drainage. They will tolerate acid or alkaline soil. They need full sun to grow dense and full but will withstand light shade. Water the plants until well established. After that, they should be able to withstand drought with little watering.

Troubleshooting

Occasionally spider mites attack Chinese hollies. See page 125 for more about spider mites.

Japanese Holly

Japanese holly is the parent species of some of the best-known evergreen shrubs. Vastly different from the wide-leafed, spiny Chinese hollies, Japanese hollies have small leaves and no spines. They offer lustrous dark green foliage, fine texture, and rapid growth and are indispensable for sunny foundation plantings.

In the Landscape

These are not flashy plants, but their reliable evergreen color and neat form throughout the year make them valuable garden tools and they are often substituted for boxwoods in hot sites. Because of their small leaves, vigorous growth, and dense branching, Japanese hollies are often used for sheared hedges.

Larger selections, such as Compacta, work well in foundations. The low-growing selections, such as Helleri, make superb ground covers, eventually growing together in a lumpy mass.

Planting and Care

Japanese hollies prefer full sun but will also grow in light shade. Good drainage is critical or plants will suffer root rot. In fact, the shrubs do best in areas where the soil is light, such as sand or sandy loam, and slightly acid. While these plants are very sturdy, you should not let them dry out. This is especially true of Helleri holly and Compacta holly. If a Japanese holly gets so dry that its leaves begin to drop, it is almost certain to die.

Japanese holly is popular for foundation plantings as it is neat and compact.

AT A GLANCE
❖
JAPANESE HOLLY
Ilex crenata

Features: fine-textured foliage, predictable form
Foliage: evergreen
Height: 2 to 10 feet
Width: 4 to 12 feet
Light: partial to full sun
Soil: loose, light textured, well drained
Water: moderate
Range: Zones 5 to 7
Pests: spider mites
Remarks: a durable evergreen for framing a landscape

Yaupon has nearly translucent red berries.

Different Selections

Compacta is a dark green globe that reaches 6 feet in height and is frequently substituted for boxwood; its new stems are purple. You will appreciate this selection's combination of dressy look, tenacity, and low cost when compared to boxwood.

Convexa is a vase-shaped, densely branched selection that grows 6 feet tall and wide. It works well as a hedge.

Helleri is mistakenly thought of as growing only 1 to 2 feet tall and equally wide, but it can ultimately grow to 4 feet tall and up to 6 feet wide, albeit slowly. It is dense and compact and makes an excellent ground cover or a substitute for dwarf boxwood.

Hetzii is a fast-growing selection, reaching 4 to 6 feet (or more) with high, loose, almost upward-angled branches, which make an economical low hedge.

Kingsville Green Cushion is a dense selection that works well as a low hedge and has a more flattened form than Helleri holly.

Troubleshooting

Spider mites will attack the plants. See page 125 for more information about spider mites.

Japanese hollies, especially Compacta, sometimes die back when planted in heavy clay, particularly when they have gone through extremes of dry and wet weather. Plant in well-drained soil and give the plants regular waterings to prevent the problem.

Yaupon Holly

Yaupon holly is a sturdy, evergreen native shrub that is often trained to be a small tree by the removal of its lower limbs, which reveals its sculptural form and handsome, silver-gray bark. The twiggy nature of the shrub makes it look very rugged and weatherworn. You can always identify a yaupon holly by its fruit, as it is the only holly with translucent berries. These ¼-inch fruits hang in clusters on the plant until spring.

Different Selections in the Landscape

Selections include the upright, treelike forms and both dwarf and weeping variations of the 15-foot native. All share characteristic finely textured foliage that is a lustrous dark green.

Yaupon has a dense growth habit that makes a very effective screen or hedge, particularly at the beach, as this coastal native is not bothered by salt spray. Large yaupon hollies can be used as an upright evergreen hedge or an accent tree to shade a patio.

Few yaupon hollies are sold by specific selection name. However, you will find a few named selections, including Pride of Houston, a selection prized for its abundant berries.

Weeping yaupon (*Ilex vomitoria* Pendula), also called Grey's weeping yaupon, is a narrow shrub that may reach 15 to 20 feet in height. Its fruit is a cascade of berries in winter, unlike anything else in the garden. The weeping habit and berry show definitely make this an eye-catching accent plant. Because it has a narrow crown, weeping yaupon is a good evergreen for small gardens and narrow areas where height is needed. It also makes an excellent specimen for a large container. Weeping yaupon's branches and stems grow rigidly downward in a stiff and sculptural manner. Often you can see right through the shrub, as its branches are thin and sparse, but the fruit is prolific and turns this into a spectacular plant.

Dwarf yaupon (*Ilex vomitoria* Nana), which forms a rounded cushion, makes a superb ground cover or foundation plant much like Japanese holly. However, dwarf yaupon holly is much more heat and drought tolerant. It is often a good substitute for boxwood or Japanese holly, especially in the heat of the deep South.

Schellings Dwarf, also known as Stokes Dwarf, is a low-growing selection (3 to 4 feet tall) that is more compact and has smaller leaves than Nana. Its young stems and leaves have a slight purple hue that often turns darker in winter.

The trunk of yaupon holly reveals an interesting coloration when the shrub's lower limbs are removed.

Planting and Care

Yaupon thrives in Zones 7 to 9, with its native range extending from the Mid-Atlantic to Texas, typically close to the coast. It will grow in almost any conditions, from the sandy soil of beaches to the richer soil of swamps, either acid or alkaline. It loves sun and heat. Once established it is very dependable and is tolerant of drought. Although rugged and tolerant of poor conditions, the larger yaupon hollies will reward you with fast growth, often a foot or more a year, if you give them rich soil and plenty of water.

Troubleshooting

Yaupon holly is not troubled by pests. However, it does have brittle branches; do not plant dwarf selections in areas where they are likely to be stepped on or hit by a wayward ball.

A mass of dwarf yaupon is pruned to mimic the undulations of the ocean beyond.

Hydrangea

Cone-shaped flowers and dramatic, coarse foliage characterize oakleaf hydrangea.

Refreshing, inviting, and long lasting, hydrangeas are dependable, old-fashioned favorites. These coarse-textured deciduous shrubs explode with color at the peak of summer.

Hydrangeas are, for the most part, large, rambling plants that need a lot of space. Used singly or in mass, they are often planted exclusively for their flowering show. Except for oakleaf hydrangea, which has year-round attributes, hydrangeas should be positioned so that they will be out of sight after the growing season.

Planting and Care

While hydrangeas will grow in full sun, they grow best when shielded from harsh afternoon rays, particularly in the lower and coastal South. In cooler regions, French, Annabelle, and oakleaf hydrangeas will grow in full sun. Peegee will grow in full sun in any region.

Plant hydrangeas in moist, well-drained, acid soil that is rich in organic matter. French and Annabelle hydrangeas need a lot of water during summer. Oakleaf hydrangea is more likely to survive drought.

Pruning

Hydrangeas benefit from pruning, but you must prune them at the right times. Prune French hydrangea immediately after it blooms; this shrub blooms from the growth of the previous season, so new growth in July will produce flowers the following May.

Prune peegee hydrangea and Annabelle hydrangea in late winter or early spring. Cut stems back to leave one or two buds and thin older canes to keep these vigorous forms under control.

Troubleshooting

Very few conditions trouble hydrangeas, though too much sun or a soggy planting site can encourage insects and diseases.

Oakleaf Hydrangea

Oakleaf hydrangea has a loose, irregular form and a mounding growth habit. Native to the shady woodlands of the Southeast, oakleaf hydrangea grows at a moderate rate to a height of 10 feet and an equal spread. Often the roots will spread to create great tangled colonies of shrubs.

The foliage of oakleaf hydrangea gradually turns deep red in fall.

The flowers appear in early summer and nearly cover the plant with 6- to 12-inch panicles of white. The oaklike leaves may be 8 to 12 inches or more in length and are deeply lobed with a very coarse texture. In the growing season they are medium green, turning brilliant colors that range from brownish red to scarlet in late fall.

When the leaves are gone, oakleaf hydrangea reveals its twisting stems and attractive peeling bark. In the latter part of fall, the flowers turn a handsome brown.

In the Landscape

Use oakleaf hydrangea in mass plantings (spaced at least 8 feet apart) to create a sweeping border for a lawn or a driveway. Since they thrive in shade, these plants mix well with rhododendron and mountain laurel. Plant them in front of white pine or Canadian hemlock to display their flowers and bark against an evergreen backdrop.

Different Selections

There are few named selections of oakleaf hydrangea. Snowflake is prized for its extra-large panicles that may be up to 1½ feet long.

Snowhill Hydrangea

Snowhill hydrangea is one of the most cold-hardy hydrangeas, growing in the Midwest and New England. It has wide panicles of white flowers that are initially borne on upright stems that gradually bend from their own weight. The flowers appear in early summer and may be as wide as 10 inches. The foliage is large and coarsely textured, closely resembling that of French hydrangea.

Old-fashioned Snowhill hydrangea, sometimes called Hills of Snow, echoes earlier generations of gardening.

AT A GLANCE
❖
SNOWHILL HYDRANGEA
Hydrangea arborescens
Grandiflora

Features: tremendous flowers in early to midsummer
Foliage: deciduous
Height: 3 to 5 feet
Width: 3 to 5 feet
Light: sun to partial shade
Soil: rich, well drained, slightly acid
Water: moderate
Range: Zones 4 to 8
Pests: none specific
Remarks: best for an informal, naturalistic design

*Annabelle hydrangea blooms turn green
again in late summer.*

In the Landscape

Snowhill hydrangea works best as a solitary specimen for a summer
accent and will reach nearly 8 feet in height. Give it a backdrop, such
as a wall or a fence. Its informal character can be unruly for small
gardens, such as a structured courtyard, but the shrub works well in
naturalistic settings.

Annabelle Hydrangea

Although related to Snowhill hydrangea, Annabelle hydrangea is
more refined and better suited to formal garden settings. As cold
hardy as Snowhill, it grows rapidly and will mature at about 5 feet
tall. The large domed flower clusters open late in the season and can
show three different hues: first apple green, fading to brilliant white,
back to green, and as the season cools, blushing to a pinkish beige.

Annabelle hydrangea's appeal is the consistency of the flowers, which rise on stout stems high above the foliage. These blooms
are good for cutting and drying.

In the Landscape

Annabelle hydrangea can be a lovely anchor for a walled garden or a
flower border in partial shade. Use it to fill the narrow, awkward
space between a sidewalk or a driveway and a wall.

You may treat Annabelle hydrangea as a perennial by pruning
it in late winter or early spring. Cut stems back to one or two buds by
snipping the canes just above a bud.

AT A GLANCE

❖

ANNABELLE HYDRANGEA

Hydrangea arborescens
Annabelle

Features: blooms from midsummer to fall

Foliage: deciduous

Height: 3 to 5 feet

Width: 3 to 5 feet

Light: partial shade

Soil: rich, well drained,
slightly acid

Water: moderate

Range: Zones 3 to 9

Pests: none specific

Remarks: treat like a perennial
by cutting it back

A massive plant with weighty flower heads, peegee hydrangea needs room to grow. It will reward you with the latest summer show of all hydrangeas.

Peegee Hydrangea

Peegee hydrangea is also a cold-hardy hydrangea and, consequently, has widespread popularity throughout the East. A rapid and vigorous grower, peegee hydrangea can easily reach 20 feet tall if left alone; however, it is often pruned to grow as a small tree, slightly more than 10 feet tall, with a single trunk.

Peegee hydrangea bears clusters of white flowers in mid-July, with each new cane ending in a foot-long cluster that is at least 8 inches wide. The weight of the flowers will cause the branches to bend, giving it a weeping aspect. The blooms are light green, maturing to white and then fading to a pinkish bronze. By September the blooms turn brown and should be removed to let the plant recede into the landscape.

In the Landscape

Peegee hydrangea is quite large and can be difficult to use. Plant lower growing evergreens in front of the shrub and allow its arching, flower-covered canes to spill over, or use it as a specimen beside a fence, an outbuilding, or any location where it can recede when not in bloom. On larger properties, the plant is spectacular when used as an informal deciduous hedge.

The plant will blend well with either needle-leafed or broad-leafed evergreens.

Annabelle hydrangea is best used as a perennial, cut back each year to provide prolific blooms. The huge flower clusters dry well for arrangements.

AT A GLANCE

❖

PEEGEE HYDRANGEA
Hydrangea paniculata
Grandiflora

Features: large white flower heads in summer
Foliage: deciduous
Height: 10 to 20 feet
Width: 10 feet
Light: full sun
Soil: rich, well drained, slightly acid
Water: moderate
Range: Zones 3 to 8
Pests: none specific
Remarks: may be trained into a treelike specimen

French hydrangea is pink if the soil is neutral to alkaline and blue if the soil is acid.

French Hydrangea

French hydrangea, a standard in the South, thrives in the heat of summer and provides weeks of garden color in white and various shades of blue, pink, and lavender. It is prized as one of the largest and brightest blues for the garden and is valued even more for its show in the shade.

French hydrangea, a coarse-textured shrub, has wide, rough leaves that are a rich green. In early summer, the top of the plant is covered with massive flowers that last for almost two months. This shrub grows 3 to 6 feet tall and equally wide but can be kept lower by pruning after it blooms.

The flowers occur in two different arrangements. The selections are divided into two groups according to the flower heads: hortensia, which is the familiar large, rounded clusters, and lacecap, which is open-flowered and less common. Lacecap selections bear tiny flowers that look like unopened buds and are ringed by large, purely ornamental flowers. Lacecaps will naturalize better than hortensias and are more refined in appearance.

Lacecap selections of French hydrangea have a more delicate-looking flower head.

In the Landscape

Use a single plant for an accent in a border or use a mass of the brightly colored flowers to brighten an area of light shade.

French hydrangea sets buds on the previous season's growth. Severe winter weather may kill the plant back to the ground; while this will rarely destroy the plant, the shoots that emerge from the base of the plant will not bloom until very late summer, if at all.

French hydrangea greets summer with huge bouquets that vary from deep pink to deep blue.

Climbing hydrangea lives up to its name by attaching itself to and climbing up structures in a vinelike fashion.

Color Changes

The blooms of French hydrangea will change color according to the pH of the soil and the amount of aluminum in the soil. Acid soil (pH of 5.0 to 5.5) produces blue flowers, while nearly neutral or alkaline soil (pH of 6.5 to 7.5) results in pink blossoms.

To maintain a blue color, sprinkle 2 tablespoons of aluminum sulfate around the roots of each plant in spring and again in fall. For pink blooms, sprinkle one cup of ground dolomitic limestone around the roots.

Different Selections

Selections of the hortensia type are often chosen for their rich color (provided the soil conditions have the appropriate pH). They include All Summer Beauty and Nikko Blue, both rich blues; Carmen and Red Star are very deep pinks. Among the popular lacecap types are Blue Bird, Blue Wave, and Mariesii.

Climbing Hydrangea

Climbing hydrangea is quite remarkable as it is a true vine, covering walls and fences with deep green foliage and clusters of white blooms in midsummer. It can climb by means of tiny aerial roots that adhere to most surfaces. The leaves drop in fall to reveal peeling cinnamon-colored bark.

Although it grows slowly at first, climbing hydrangea makes rapid progress when established, growing as tall as the support allows but with the capacity to climb 60 feet. The vine does not stay flat against its support but projects branches outward, as though becoming a living scaffold.

In the Landscape

Use climbing hydrangea either as a ground cover around a natural rock feature or as the ornamental vine on a stone wall. It may also be used in courtyards as a feature planting. Be sure that you plant it where it can be trimmed back easily if needed. Climbing hydrangea is also better suited for a surface that will not need to be painted.

AT A GLANCE
❖
CLIMBING HYDRANGEA
Hydrangea anomala petiolaris

Features: clusters of white flowers, cinnamon-colored bark

Foliage: deciduous

Height: up to 60 feet

Width: varies

Light: partial shade

Soil: rich, well drained, slightly acid

Water: moderate

Range: Zones 4 to 7

Pests: none specific

Remarks: a unique climber for walls and fences

Kerria

Pleniflora features full, double blossoms against the characteristic green stems and crisp-looking foliage of the plant.

The tumbling golden blossoms of old-fashioned Japanese kerria offer a bright salute among spring's youthful greens. This shrub is one of the few plants that bloom well in shade. When the spring show is over, kerria will continue to produce a handful of sporadic blooms through summer, and its slender, bright green stems hold their color all year long.

In the Landscape

A rangy, arching shrub, Japanese kerria grows 5 to 8 feet tall and at least as wide. If left alone, it will creep and spread via suckers to fill a 12-foot-wide space; it makes an excellent background for azaleas, rhododendrons, small woodland flowers, and understory trees. Kerria also dresses up shrub borders and cottage gardens.

On a large lot, kerria is useful for a distant mass planting where you can enjoy the 1- to 2-inch-wide golden yellow blooms in spring and use its green as a backdrop for other seasonal color throughout the year. To enjoy its green stems and rangy form, place kerria where it has a backdrop such as a stone wall or a fence. Because of its loose, open form, kerria also works well in a rustic setting.

Planting and Care

Bright, direct sun makes the flowers fade quickly, so select a planting site in partial shade. Japanese kerria prefers moist, well-drained soil that is rich in organic matter, but once established, the plant will survive in the dry shade under the canopy of large trees.

Arching sprays of Japanese kerria brighten a shady area.

AT A GLANCE
❖
JAPANESE KERRIA
Kerria japonica

Features: yellow spring flowers, upright growth

Foliage: deciduous

Height: 5 to 8 feet

Width: 5 to 12 feet

Light: partial sun to shade

Soil: moist, well drained, loamy

Water: moderate

Range: Zones 4 to 9

Pests: none serious

Remarks: brings dependable spring bloom for shade

The simplicity of its single blooms gives this Japanese kerria a soft look.

Prune dead stems or old woody stems by removing them at the base of the plant. To keep kerria from spreading, remove suckers from the base by digging them with a shovel. You may do this at any time, but fall and winter are the best seasons to dig if you want to plant the suckers elsewhere.

Different Selections

Pleniflora has double flowers that are nearly spherical. It is both showier and taller than the parent species though not as dense. It grows into a tumbling mound of foliage and flowers. Picta has leaves that are edged with white and brightens the shade even when the plant is not in bloom; its flowers are single and are not as full as those of Pleniflora, but some gardeners prefer the simplicity of these blooms. Shannon is a green-leafed selection with single yellow flowers that are a bit larger than those of other selections.

Troubleshooting

Too much fertilizer will give you abundant foliage but few flowers. Japanese kerria needs little or no extra feeding.

The flowers of Japanese kerria also come in single form.

Ligustrum

The tenacity of ligustrum makes it excellent for severe conditions, such as those caused by the reflected heat of a brick wall.

Ligustrum is a genuine landscape bargain. Undaunted by heat or poor soil, this shrub has excellent long-term garden value as an inexpensive, fast-growing, and long-lived evergreen. Gardeners in the coastal regions of the deep South and Texas know the usefulness of this plant and its ability to grow in poor sandy soil.

Sometimes called Japanese or waxleaf privet, this shrub will grow quickly to 10 to 12 feet. It may reach 18 feet tall in tropical climates, where it is often trained into a small tree. The plant has an upright rounded form and is covered with dark green, 1½- to 4-inch-long leaves. The leaves remain steadily green throughout the year. In late spring and early summer, large panicles of tiny white flowers emerge from the tips of the branches. The flowers mature into small blue fruits that will persist through winter.

The sculptural branch structure and gray-brown, dotted bark are very attractive when the lower foliage is pruned away to form a treelike shrub.

In the Landscape

Ligustrum is valuable for its landscape versatility. It may be used as a single specimen, a container plant, a dense privacy planting, a sheared hedge, or a tree-form patio plant.

The ultimate size of the plant is the most important consideration for its landscape use. Left unpruned, ligustrum will quickly provide a landscape backdrop for more ornamental flowering shrubs. However, it is often pruned into a tall formal hedge or simply left to

---

AT A GLANCE

❖

LIGUSTRUM

Ligustrum japonicum

Features: glossy dark green foliage, white flower spikes

Foliage: evergreen

Height: 6 to 18 feet

Width: 6 to 8 feet

Light: full sun

Soil: well drained

Water: moderate

Range: Zones 7 to 10

Pests: none specific

Remarks: an attractive, versatile evergreen

grow, creating a free-form informal screen. Remove the lower branches to create a small evergreen tree that is about the same size as a small crape myrtle; these tree-form plants are popular accents in beds of flowers or ground cover.

Planting and Care

Ligustrum transplants readily and is extremely tolerant of difficult growing conditions; it thrives in soils ranging from heavy clay to light sand. It will grow in either sun or shade. Because it tolerates severe heat, ligustrum is a superb evergreen for the hottest, driest climates, almost thriving on neglect.

Different Selections

Although most of the plants you find will simply be labeled ligustrum, there are a few named selections. Variegatum has leaves with a creamy yellow margin. Rotundifolium is a slow-growing curiosity, reaching only 4 feet in height. It has rounded, almost contorted, dark green leaves that closely wrap the branches as though they were melted plastic; use this plant strictly as an accent.

Ligustrum is a reliable container plant and an inexpensive living sculpture.

The sculptural branching of a tree-form ligustrum is paired with a garden statue to make an accent for a garden walkway.

89

Loropetalum

Loropetalum responds well to pruning and is easily trained onto a wall as an espalier.

Loropetalum is a medium-sized evergreen shrub that will spark conversation with its curious fringelike flowers. The flower show is captivating both when viewed up close and from far away, covering the shrub with finely cut, creamy white tassels in early spring. A bonus of these fleecy flowers is that they are mildly fragrant.

The dainty blooms contrast with loropetalum's vigorous growth, which rewards gardeners who have room to grow this shrub and are looking for quick effect. Ultimately growing to 6 to 15 feet tall and equally wide, a small 1-gallon plant will easily reach 5 feet in height in 3 to 4 years, provided good planting conditions. The leaves are 1 to 2½ inches long; they are dark green and rough on the top and lighter colored on the underside.

In the Landscape

Set loropetalum aside to fill a corner of a walled garden or to block an unwanted view. Though medium to fine in texture, loropetalum is not dressy and looks best when used in a naturalized setting. In formal locations, it looks slightly unruly but can be dressed up wonderfully by contrasting it with more manicured plants, such as pittosporum or cleyera. You may also train it as an espalier.

Loropetalum is perfect for a large, informal screen or hedge beneath light shade and can be successfully shaped into a small tree by having the lower branches pruned. At first, plants tend to be low and spreading but later send up branches that cause the plant to assume a surprising upright form.

Planting and Care

Loropetalum will adjust to many different conditions but must have well-drained, slightly acid soil that is rich in organic matter. Moisture should be constant. Loropetalum prefers full sun but you can move it to partial shade and it will do just fine.

This shrub takes any amount of pruning well.

Different Selections

Burgundy is a selection with pink flowers and dark red leaves. You may find other selections of loropetalum with pink flowers and dark burgundy-red foliage, but most of the white-flowered selections are simply sold by the species name.

A fast-growing evergreen, loropetalum reaches an imposing size in just a few years and blooms for two to three weeks each spring.

Mahonia

AT A GLANCE
❖
LEATHERLEAF MAHONIA
Mahonia bealei

Features: sculptural form, yellow flowers, purple-blue fruit

Foliage: evergreen

Height: 6 to 10 feet

Width: 6 to 8 feet

Light: partial shade

Soil: moist, rich, acid, well drained

Water: moderate

Range: Zones 6 to 9

Pests: none specific

Remarks: a durable living sculpture

Bright yellow flowers emerge from the tips of leatherleaf mahonia very early in the year.

The form and foliage of mahonia make these the most architectural plants for any garden. Each plant is a collection of several canes (like those of nandina) that reach from the ground to sport lengthy leaves, each with 9 to 13 hollylike leaflets, atop its stems.

Spikes of bright yellow citrus-scented blooms form at the tops of the stems in late winter or early spring. In summer, large clusters of powdery purple-blue berries remain on the plant until they are eaten by birds.

Leatherleaf Mahonia

Leatherleaf mahonia is the largest of this group, reaching 6 to 10 feet in height and 6 to 8 feet in spread. This slow- to moderate-growing shrub is a cluster of canes and glossy, blue-green foliage.

In the Landscape

Entry courtyards with strong architectural features are excellent locations for the line and form of leatherleaf mahonia. Place it in front of a textured stone wall or a wooden fence, or use it as the singular planting above a dark-bottomed pool. Use leatherleaf mahonia in a bed of ground cover or to punctuate the rounded form and softer foliage of azaleas. You may also plant it in small clusters of about three plants to create a small grove in a corner of a foundation planting. It also works well at the edge of a deck to act as an airy evergreen screen to help block the view below.

Planting and Care

Leatherleaf mahonia grows best in light shade and prefers moist, well-drained, slightly acid soil that is rich in organic matter. Avoid full sun as the leaves will lose their dark glossy color; however, three to four hours of early morning sun will encourage blooming. Also avoid locations that are subject to drying winter winds.

Different Selections

Leatherleaf mahonia is sold simply as the species.

Troubleshooting

There are no serious insects or diseases that affect the plant.

The sculptural form of leatherleaf mahonia stands as a green garden sculpture.

Leatherleaf mahonia produces grapelike clusters of berries in summer.

AT A GLANCE
❖
OREGON GRAPE HOLLY
Mahonia aquifolium

Features:, yellow flowers, blue-black fruit

Foliage: evergreen

Height: 3 to 6 feet

Width: 3 to 5 feet

Light: partial shade to shade

Soil: moist, rich, acid, well drained

Water: moderate

Range: Zones 4 to 8

Pests: none specific

Remarks: a fine shrub for shady settings

As a group, mahonias are known for their sculptural habit and spiny, hollylike leaves.

Oregon Grape Holly

The smallest of the mahonias, Oregon grape holly will turn bright ruby red in winter. Also, the plant is **stoloniferous,** spreading underground to form a colony of stems topped with foliage that may be as much as 6 feet wide. The shrub grows slowly to an eventual height of 6 feet but maintains a compact form.

The spiny leaflets are 1½ to 3½ inches long; there are five to nine leaflets per leaf. Oregon grape holly's yellow flowers are borne in early spring, appearing snugly against the stems of the plant. The fruit is blue black but inconspicuous.

In the Landscape

Oregon grape holly may be tucked into niches of a landscape—between a footpath and a wall or in an elevated planter—without the dramatic imposition of leather-leaf mahonia. Use the plant as a coarse-textured contrast amid softer plants, such as Gumpo azaleas. The small size of Oregon grape holly makes it suitable for combination with ferns beneath a birdbath or as an accent plant in conjunction with an opening in a rock wall.

Planting and Care

Plant Oregon grape holly in light shade and in moist, well-drained, slightly acid soil that is rich in organic matter. Partial shade all day is best. Shelter the plant from drying winter winds.

Species and Selections

Atropurpureum has dark reddish-purple leaves in winter. Compactum, a dwarf selection, remains under 2 feet tall. Golden Abundance has profuse, large flowers and more fruit than other selections. Orange Flame has bronze-orange new foliage.

A related species, cluster mahonia *(Mahonia pinnata)*, tolerates more sun than other mahonias but still requires protection from direct summer sun. This shrub does best in Zones 7 and 8 but does not like extremes of heat or cold.

Cluster mahonia spreads underground to create colonies of tall, stemmy plants that may reach 5 to 7 feet, though they are usually smaller. The foliage is spiny with a blue-gray color and turns deep purple in winter. It has yellow flowers followed by bluish-black fruit. Cluster mahonia is more suited to a mass planting in the landscape because it spreads rapidly and fills a large area.

Troubleshooting

There are no serious pests and diseases.

In winter, cluster mahonia turns deep purple.

Mountain Laurel

Mountain laurel typically has pink flower buds that unfold to five-sided flowers.

The cool, moist Eastern forests are home to this magnificent and durable evergreen. An indisputably handsome shrub in any season, mountain laurel explodes into bloom in late spring or early summer to light up the shade with bell-like blooms.

The 1-inch-wide, five-sided flowers emerge light pink from deeper pink buds and open to reveal purple markings dappled around the inside. These distinctive flecks of color give the shrub the nickname calico bush.

This tough, adaptable, medium-textured plant grows slowly into a gnarly-trunked mound of glossy foliage about 15 feet tall and equally wide. The bark is deep brown and is textured with fine lines.

In the Landscape

Mountain laurel makes a superb specimen or mass planting for shady settings. This versatility is offset by one drawback: it grows very slowly. Even in the warmer parts of its native range (which stretches from Canada to north Florida) mountain laurel lags behind rhododendron, deciduous azalea, and oakleaf hydrangea, its companion plants.

This slow growth contributes to the irregular form and sculptural nature of the plant, the trait that makes it an elegant specimen. In the wild, plants spread from a dominant trunk that has a gnarled, contorted look. Plants with multiple trunks are more common in the nursery trade and will grow to form a more rounded, symmetrical mass in the garden.

Planted in masses, mountain laurel may create a very dense evergreen screen, but it is not the plant for an urgent solution to a landscape eyesore. These plants look best when naturalized and have an especially attractive appeal when used with rocks.

Plant it where you will not have to prune it—it should not be cut except to remove dead or damaged wood. You may snip off spent flower heads in order to encourage more blooms.

Planting and Care

If you can mimic the native conditions that it prefers—moist, well-drained, rich, acid soil—mountain laurel will thrive in your garden. Mulch, preferably shredded leaves, is a must to help the plant withstand drought and to allow the shallow feeder roots to spread.

AT A GLANCE
❖
MOUNTAIN LAUREL
Kalmia latifolia

Features: elegant foliage, unpredictable form, clusters of flowers

Foliage: evergreen

Height: 7 to 15 feet

Width: 7 to 15 feet

Light: shade to partial shade

Soil: moist, rich, acid, well drained

Water: moderate

Range: Zones 4 to 8

Pests: leaf spot

Remarks: one of the best flowering evergreens for shade

In spite of its normally shady setting, mountain laurel has a high tolerance for direct sun, which will increase blooming. Mountain laurel may struggle in gardens in Zone 8 despite the fact that the plant occurs naturally in this area.

Different Selections

Several selections offer different attributes than the species. Alba has pure white flowers. Myrtifolia is a compact form that remains under 6 feet tall. Pink Charm has red flower buds that are rich pink when they first open. Rubra has deep pink flowers. The blooms of Shooting Star have deeply cut, reflexed lobes.

Troubleshooting

Mountain laurel may occasionally be bothered by the insects that attack rhododendrons and evergreen azaleas (see pages 45 and 106).

Leaf spot may disfigure the foliage and cause the leaves to drop. If you see spots on the foliage, contact your local Extension agent for a recommended control.

A loose, irregularly shaped shrub that is showered with clusters of flowers, mountain laurel is among the finest evergreens for any garden. After opening, the pink flowers of mountain laurel fade to white.

Nandina

In winter, nandina is covered with brilliant red berries.

AT A GLANCE
❖

NANDINA
Nandina domestica

Features: delicate foliage, profuse winter fruit

Foliage: evergreen

Height: 1½ to 8 feet

Width: 3 to 4 feet

Light: full sun to shade

Soil: moist, rich, well drained, slightly acid

Water: moderate

Range: Zones 6 to 9

Pests: none specific

Remarks: delicate looking but very tough

The delicate foliage of nandina belies its rugged durability as an adaptable, versatile evergreen. This shrub is ideal for problem areas in sun or shade, especially small, confined spaces. Nandina needs only an occasional snip with pruning shears to assume the marvelously stalky, fine-textured form that inspired another common name, heavenly bamboo.

Spreading from underground rhizomes, nandina grows at a moderate rate to reach approximately 8 feet tall but rarely more than 4 feet wide. The plant's form is upright and stemmy; it is a collection of woody canes sporting finely divided compound leaves.

In late spring, large panicles of small white flowers emerge from the tops of the foliage-covered canes. The flowers mature into green berries that are ¼ inch in diameter and hang in 8-inch clusters. The fruit turns brilliant red in early fall and remains on the shrub through the winter.

The foliage varies in color with age, location, and season. The young foliage emerges copper colored before maturing to bright green. In shady sites the mature foliage is a dark blue green, but in the sun the foliage has a reddish color, a hue that deepens in the winter.

In the Landscape

Strongly architectural in character, nandina's fine texture contrasts handsomely with materials as varied as stacked stone, clapboard siding, or wooden fencing. It is also effective as an accent against stucco or tabby walls. Use it in borders of shrubs or perennials, or place it adjacent to a patio or sitting area. Plant dwarf selections as a ground cover. Nandina is also ideal for tight spaces, such as the confines between a patio and courtyard wall or a narrow sidewalk and the house.

Nandina combines well with horizontally spreading evergreens, such as cotoneaster, or mounding evergreens, such as Indian hawthorn or Helleri holly.

Planting and Care

Although nandina grows best in fertile, slightly acid, well-drained soil, it will also grow in poor soils if provided adequate drainage. After it is established, nandina is very drought tolerant. Keep young plants watered, however, until they are rooted in their new locations.

Nandina should not be pruned other than to thin its density and lower its height; do this only if desired. Remove the oldest, longest canes in early spring by cutting them at ground level. To keep the plants full for use as a screen, cut several canes at various heights from the base of the plant. Cut a few at ground level; then cut more about one-third along the height of the plant, and then again two-thirds along the height of the plant. This will encourage a fuller plant.

Different Selections

There are many selections of nandina. Alba is a creamy white form. Nana Purpurea has softer looking foliage and vivid red fall color. Compacta stays less than 4 feet tall; Harbour Dwarf grows to 3 feet tall and has perfect foliage and a very full form. Woods Dwarf spreads rapidly underground and makes a good ground cover. Gulf Stream is a slow-growing, dense form that reaches about 4 feet in height. Orihime has very thin, threadlike leaves and grows only 1½ to 2 feet tall.

Nandina is a delicately textured shrub that can be used in foundation plantings or as an accent.

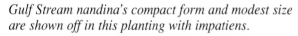

Gulf Stream nandina's compact form and modest size are shown off in this planting with impatiens.

Pittosporum

Wheeler's Dwarf pittosporum rarely grows taller than 4 feet, a workable height for foundation plantings.

Pittosporum is recognized for its crisp, dense foliage and tolerance to extremes of heat and drought. It can withstand the heat of full sun and reflected sunlight, as well as the harsh salt spray of the beach.

These are invariably neat plants—no pruning required—and the species is a steady grower, slowly sprawling to its mature height. The thick evergreen leaves are whorled at the ends of the branches and densely cover the plant. The leathery leaves are about 3 inches long, are rounded at the tips, and tend to curl under along the sides. In spring, tiny white to pale yellow flowers are inconspicuous but very fragrant.

Different Selections in the Landscape

Japanese pittosporum is the largest pittosporum, growing to 10 feet in height and up to 15 feet in width. Its mature size requires a large space in the garden. This is a very effective shrub for a privacy planting, a use that takes advantage of its height and spread and the fact that it branches to the ground.

Consider Japanese pittosporum as an anchor plant in the corner of a garden. In a small space, you may prune the lower branches to create a treelike specimen; silhouette the trunk against a wall or a fence. When the shrub is in bloom, its fragrance will fill a courtyard.

Variegata, called whitespot Japanese pittosporum, makes a bright accent in a lightly shaded location, such as along a garden edge in the shadow of tall pines. Play its brighter foliage against the darker, coarser foliage of holly or viburnum. Use it beside an entry

---

AT A GLANCE
❖
PITTOSPORUM
Pittosporum tobira

Features: neat form, fragrant flowers, drought tolerant

Foliage: evergreen

Height: 3 to 10 feet

Width: 4 to 15 feet

Light: full sun to shade

Soil: well drained, sandy

Water: low

Range: Zone 8 to 10

Pests: none specific

Remarks: sturdy, neat evergreen for hot climates and the beach

or adjacent to a terrace to lighten the garden setting, keeping in mind that this selection is also very large.

Wheeler's Dwarf pittosporum is the most popular pittosporum, a dwarf selection (3 feet tall and 4 feet wide) that is a good foundation plant. The distinctive gray-green leaves are margined in a creamy white, making this an unusually light-colored shrub. Place it in front of larger, darker evergreens, such as ligustrum or Sandankwa viburnum. Its mounding form and limited height make it an ideal shrub for the corner of a foundation or a shrub border. It requires no pruning to control its size yet adds enough dimension and texture to fill a garden space. Use Wheeler's Dwarf pittosporum as the background plant for low-growing annuals and perennials. It also makes a splendid potted plant.

Planting and Care

Pittosporum will grow in hot, full sun and is also a successful, full plant in heavy shade. It grows very well in poor, sandy soil but will also grow in clay, provided it has adequate drainage. It also tolerates salt spray and is often used in beachfront plantings.

Protect this shrub from severe winter winds; sustained temperatures below 15 to 20 degrees and drying winds will burn the plant. Where there has been cold damage, light pruning usually restores pittosporum to good form and vigor.

Pittosporum also thrives in containers and as a patio plant.

Pyracantha

In late spring, pyracantha is wrapped in clusters of white flowers.

An erratically branching evergreen that quickly soars as tall as 18 feet, pyracantha is draped in clusters of white flowers in mid-spring, followed with a blaze of fruit in fall.

In summer, its narrow, elliptic leaves are lustrous and give the plant a fine texture. If left alone to grow naturally, pyracantha becomes an erratically branching, upright, spreading plant. The mature shrub is as wide as or wider than it is tall.

The beauty of this shrub comes with a price that is warned by the name *pyracantha,* which means firethorn. The shrub is sometimes called scarlet firethorn and is armed with long, sharp spines that are ½ to ¾ inch long. Fortunately, hybridization has tamed this shrub. There are many selections that are more manageable in size and are less thorny than the parent plant.

In the Landscape

The irregular, open form of pyracantha calls for a large space in the garden. This precludes foundation plantings except for high, windowless walls or brick structures, such as a chimney. Pyracantha is also popular for espaliers.

You may use pyracantha as an accent plant against such structures as stone or brick columns, fences, and walls. A single shrub may be used to screen a small area or to disguise an unsightly view or object in the landscape; several plants may be planted as an informal hedge.

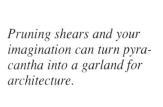

Pruning shears and your imagination can turn pyracantha into a garland for architecture.

AT A GLANCE
❖
PYRACANTHA
Pyracantha coccinea

Features: prolific flowers, orange to red berries in fall

Foliage: evergreen

Height: 6 to 18 feet

Width: 6 to 18 feet

Light: full sun

Soil: well drained

Water: low

Range: Zones 6 to 9

Pests: fire blight, scab on fruit

Remarks: an irregular evergreen with a spectacular show of berries

Planting and Care

Plant pyracantha in full sun. While it prefers rich soil, it will tolerate any soil that is not soggy; it needs good drainage. These plants love heat, even reflected light. Once established, pyracantha is exceptionally drought tolerant.

Different Selections

The many selections of pyracantha originated from different parent plants.

From scarlet firethorn *(Pyracantha coccinea)* comes Aurea, a selection with yellow berries. Kasan is very cold hardy and has red-orange fruits but is susceptible to scab. Lalandei has orange berries and upright growth to 15 or more feet. It is a spiny, hardy, and vigorous selection.

From Formosa firethorn *(Pyracantha koidzumii)* a smaller, less hardy species, comes Low-Dense, a large selection with orange-red berries and a mounding growth habit. It grows to 6 feet in height and is finely textured and unusually dressy for a pyracantha. Victory is a vigorous, upright, arching plant that grows to about 10 feet tall. Walderi Prostrata has red berries and a prostrate habit, growing only 4 feet tall; it makes a good ground cover.

New hybrid selections include Mohave, which has many flowers and huge masses of fruit; it grows to 10 feet tall. Navaho stays low (about 6 feet) and is densely branched and mounding with abundant orange-red fruit. Teton has a strong, upright growth habit and yellow-orange fruit; it grows to 16 feet tall.

Troubleshooting

The most devastating problem of pyracantha is fire blight, a bacterial disease that causes the branches to turn brown as if they have been burned. It will seriously threaten if not destroy a plant. See page 124 for more about fire blight. Scab is another disease that affects the appearance of the berries, turning them a dark sooty color.

As a landscape feature, pyracantha needs plenty of room and the companionship of a structure to look best.

Rhododendron

The large clusters of rhododendron blooms are called trusses.

AT A GLANCE
❖
RHODODENDRON
Rhododendron catawbiense

Features: handsome foliage, elegant form, huge flower trusses

Foliage: evergreen

Height: 3 to 12 feet

Width: 3 to 12 feet

Light: partial shade

Soil: organic, slightly acid, moist, well drained

Water: moderate

Range: Zones 4 to 8

Pests: lacebugs, wilt, rhododendron borers

Remarks: durable, excellent in a massed planting or as a single specimen

Gardeners choose rhododendron for its colorful flowers, but the greatest landscape attributes of this handsome evergreen shrub are its form and foliage. The steady green leaves and coarse texture of rhododendron are constant throughout the year, joined in late spring by the beautiful blooms.

Few plants pop into color like rhododendrons. A single cluster of flowers is like a round bouquet, with some clusters including as many as two dozen individual blooms. These clusters are often called **trusses.** The immense flower clusters may cover the plant, but never do they totally hide the foliage. Instead, they perch atop individual limbs like crowns. The presentation is both understated and classically beautiful. It is no wonder that these shrubs are among the most popular evergreens.

Rhododendrons are reasonably inexpensive and very durable. Their utility derives from the many sizes available and their slow, steady growth each season. The shrubs range from 3 to 12 feet in both height and width, depending on the selection. The plants grow steadily but not rapidly; each branch grows about 6 inches and adds a single whorl of 4- to 6-inch leaves each year. The top foliage reaches upward while the lower branches layer gracefully along the ground.

In the Landscape

Rhododendrons are choice shrubs for privacy plantings, for screening an undesirable view, or for creating spaces in a shady garden. Here is a general rule of thumb: if one rhododendron looks good, two or more will look better. These are good shrubs to drift in undisturbed woodlands of your property to create a sense of enclosure or privacy. Rhododendrons are impressive when placed along a driveway or used in a sweep around the edge of a lawn. They also lend a comfortable, almost tropical feel to walkways or entry courtyards, yet retain a slight formality. On average-sized lots, use rhododendron to create a back or side wall of vegetation; these shrubs will suit as the backdrop for either formal or casual plantings.

In small areas, where large sweeps are not possible, group three together in a corner of the garden. Use them to frame a terrace or patio, as the backdrop planting for a bird feeder or birdbath, or to anchor a shaded border of perennials, such as ferns and hostas.

You can blend rhododendrons with deciduous azaleas, mountain laurel, and oakleaf hydrangea, all natural companions.

Planting and Care

Rhododendrons need partial shade; the filtered shade from tall pine trees or willow oaks is ideal. Plant them where they will receive only morning sun, as they will not grow in hot afternoon sun. In full sun, their shape becomes unnaturally dense, their foliage bleaches to yellow green, and they are more susceptible to lacebugs. In deep shade, rhododendrons will not bloom profusely and the plants will stretch and look leggy as they reach for light.

The bright red flowers of this rhododendron, Vulcan, accent the entrance to a country driveway.

One of the most dependable rhododendrons is Roseum Elegans which will grow taller than 6 feet in 10 years.

Rhododendrons need rich, loose soil that is both moist and well drained. More rhododendrons die because of poor drainage than any other cause, as they are very susceptible to wilt disease in poorly drained soil. Add organic matter, such as sphagnum peat moss, composted leaf mold, or pulverized pine bark, into the soil mixture of the planting hole. In areas with heavy clay soils you may plant "high" so that the top half of the root ball is actually above ground level. Back fill is then piled up to cover the exposed sides of the root ball. After planting, be sure to mulch around the base of the shrubs.

Rhododendrons must have slightly acid soil; they will not grow in alkaline soil. The pH of your water supply may also be a factor. If the water is alkaline, you should monitor your soil pH to make sure that you maintain conditions that are favorable to rhododendrons. Often this is corrected by adding sulfur to the soil. A very low pH (4 to 4.5) also helps prevent wilt.

Different Selections

Many hybrid rhododendron selections originate from the Southern native, Catawbiense rhododendron. These selections are durable and proven; some, however, are better suited to the warmer reaches of their range than others. If you are wary of rhododendrons, start with a proven selection, such as English Roseum (lavender), Catawbiense Album (white), or Nova Zembla (red). Flower colors include white, yellow, red, and many shades of pink and purple.

As with azaleas, the rhododendrons for sale in your area will likely be the best selections for local conditions.

Troubleshooting

While rhododendrons are susceptible to the same pests as evergreen azaleas (see page 45), many problems are caused by improper planting and care. All too often, the plant's roots are allowed to stay too damp, which encourages a disease called wilt. This type of root rot causes the roots to no longer convey water and nutrients to the plant. The symptoms are wilted leaves as the plant dies from lack of water.

Rhododendrons often dry out from lack of water in summer. They signal water deprivation by drooping their leaves. It is best to keep the soil evenly moist, despite the risk of wilt.

Plants are also desiccated by prolonged exposure to cold winter winds. In very cold weather, the leaves will droop but will also curl, a confusing sign that does not necessarily mean that you need to water. If the leaves unfurl as the temperature warms, the plant is probably fine. However, browned and brittle leaf edges indicate that the plant is being "freeze-dried," or suffering from winter wind-burn. If this happens repeatedly, you will have to protect the plant from the wind-caused desiccation. You can spray the foliage with an antidesiccant to reduce damage or move it to a location that is sheltered from winter winds.

The sudden death of one limb may be a sign of rhododendron borers, beetle larvae that tunnel into the trunk and limbs. Contact your county Extension agent if you suspect an infestation.

HYBRID RHODODENDRONS FOR THE SOUTH

Flower Color	Height*		
	Tall (over 6 feet)	Medium (4 to 6 feet)	Low (under 4½ feet)
Lavender	Catawbiense Grandiflorum English Roseum Roseum Elegans	Blue Peter Blue Ensign Caroline	Sapphire (dwarf; less than 1½ feet)
Pink	Anna Rose Whitney	Countess of Derby Holden Lady Clementine Mitford Pink Cameo Van Nes Sensation Vernus	Pioneer P.J.M.
Purple		Anah Kruschke Purpureum Grandiflorum	Besse Howells
Red	Cynthia	America Nova Zembla Vulcan	Elizabeth Jean Marie de Montague
Rose		King Tut Ignatius Sargent	
White	County of York White Pearl	Belle Heller Catawbiense Album Gomer Waterer Ice Cube Mrs. Tom H. Lowinsky	Chionoides Cunningham's White (semidwarf; less than 3 feet)
Yellow		Butterfly Old Copper	Unique

*After 10 years under ideal conditions

Scotch Broom

There is nothing common about the yellow flowers of common Scotch broom.

The butter yellow flowers of Scotch broom lighten up the summer garden. This unusually eye-catching plant has inconspicuous leaves and appears to be a mass of upright green stems. The flowers are followed by pea-shaped pods, which some gardeners remove from the shrub. Scotch broom has a strong vertical habit and a plumed texture for a unique look.

In the Landscape

Because of its size (5 to 8 feet tall and 8 to 12 feet wide), Scotch broom can be used as you would use forsythia, either as a single specimen or in a large sweep. Or plant it in a shrub border, tucking it between coarser textured plants, such as viburnum. It contrasts nicely with a cascading plant, such as a cotoneaster.

The plant will become large enough to use as a screen but benefits from a backdrop, such as a wall, a fence, or tree trunks. You may also plant perennials or mounding evergreens in front of Scotch broom. Smaller hybrid selections work well in containers or as part of a perennial border.

Planting and Care

Scotch broom demands a sunny location and excellent drainage. Although it grows best in moist, well-drained soil, Scotch broom will tolerate poor, sandy, dry soil. It is normal for branches to die out as new ones emerge.

Scotch broom is covered in deep yellow flowers in mid- to late spring.

Different Species

There are several species in the broom family as they have have been extensively hybridized. Though they are considered "improved," many hybrids are less heat tolerant than the species. Warminster broom *(Cytisus* x *praecox)* is similar to Scotch broom but forms a more dense mass; some gardeners avoid it because its flowers have an odor. Moonlight grows low and wide and bears light yellow blooms. Hollandia has pink flowers; Lilac Time is a dwarf form with reddish-purple flowers.

Warminster broom is more dense than Scotch broom.

Spirea

Old-fashioned bridal wreath spirea is as lovely as a porcelain sculpture.

AT A GLANCE
❖
SPRING-FLOWERING SPIREAS
Spiraea species and hybrids

Features: profuse flowers, delicate form, low maintenance

Foliage: deciduous

Height: 6 to 8 feet

Width: 6 to 10 feet

Light: full sun

Soil: rich, well drained

Water: moderate

Range: Zones 3 to 9

Pests: none specific

Remarks: excellent where breezes can move the branches

Spireas are an old-fashioned group of shrubs that include large, spring-flowering species with white flowers and smaller, summer-flowering species with pink blooms.

All spireas are finely textured and are especially willowy at the tips of the branches. Even the individual flowers have the dainty quality of finely crafted porcelain sculpture. When the leaves fall, the branches appear to be netting in the landscape.

The dainty appearance belies spirea's hardiness and toughness. These long-lived shrubs are rugged enough to thrive on untended property.

In the Landscape

The large, spring-flowering spireas work best as billowing masses or natural hedges at the edge of a garden or along the property line. They are especially beautiful when massed on a slope. Use them to soften the side of a garage or to screen an undesirable view. The branch network will become so thick that spireas are effective screens even in winter.

While they will benefit from an evergreen backdrop, such as white pine, Norway spruce, or red cedar, the shrubs may be used singly or in masses without a backdrop. In fact, the handsome foliage and arching form make them excellent backdrop plants for a perennial border or as specimen plantings. When using these plants, be sure to give them plenty of room.

The smaller, summer-flowering spireas, such as Anthony Waterer, Goldflame, Lime Mound, and Alpine, are perfect for a perennial border or any intimate, sunny space. Blend them between blue and pink perennials or combine them with plants that have

Baby's breath spirea is the first spirea to bloom in spring.

maroon foliage, such as bloodleaf Japanese maple or Crimson Pygmy barberry. Use these delicate, low-growing selections in front of large, tropical plants, such as bronze-leafed canna lilies.

Planting and Care

Although adapted to almost any soil, including heavy clays, spireas do best in light, well-drained soil that is rich in organic matter. The shrubs can tolerate a fair amount of shade; however, the flower show is best in full sun.

Old, overgrown spireas will come back fresh and strong if you prune one-third of the branches to the ground each year for three years. Trim the longest, oldest branches first. If maintaining the form is not important, you can prune them to the ground all at once; after two scruffy-looking seasons the shrub will regain its graceful form. Spireas are often pruned incorrectly, which ruins both their form and their flower show.

To control height or to cut stems for arrangements, use hand shears to snip branches at different heights in the plant's interior. Prune spring-flowering spireas immediately after flowering. Prune summer-flowering Bumalda and Alpine spireas in late winter or early spring.

Spring-Flowering Species

There are many different species of spring-flowering spireas. Baby's breath spirea *(Spiraea thunbergii)* blooms in late winter or early spring. Distinguished by its broadly rounded, arching form and delicate, finely textured branches, baby's breath spirea is airy and dainty when covered with single white flowers. Tiny leaves follow the flowers and turn bright yellow green during the growing season. In fall the foliage is gold or bronze. Baby's breath spirea may reach a height and spread of 6 feet after many years, though 4 to 5 feet in height and width is more typical.

Bridal wreath spirea *(Spiraea prunifolia)* is an upright, vase-shaped plant with dark twigs that shoot upward. The shrub will grow to as much as 6 feet tall and 5 or 6 feet wide. Bridal wreath spirea blooms just after baby's breath spirea, opening its clusters slowly. Its propensity for early bloom and the durability of the flowers make it a good choice for forcing. The dark green, finely textured foliage of bridal wreath spirea can be quite handsome and will turn a beautiful red in fall, but the plant tends to be leggy and unkempt.

Reeves spirea is one of the dressiest and showiest of the spring-flowering group.

In fall, the fine foliage of baby's breath spirea turns a lovely golden bronze.

Reeves spirea *(Spiraea cantoniensis)* is the most elegant spirea, with handsome blue-green foliage and symmetrical form. The flowers are carried in dense, bouquet-like clusters down the length of every stem about two weeks later than baby's breath spirea. Growing to a height and spread of 4 to 5 feet, Reeves spirea, with its mounded growth habit and fine foliage, is better suited to formal or specimen uses than any other large spirea.

Vanhoutte spirea *(Spiraea* x *vanhouttei)* looks like a larger version of Reeves spirea. Frequently growing to 8 feet tall and 10 feet wide, Vanhoutte is perfect for large spaces and massing at a property's edge. Vanhoutte spirea blooms two weeks after Reeves spirea and the flowers appear in rounded clusters on the stems for a showy display.

Summer-Flowering Species

There are many different species of summer-flowering spireas. Anthony Waterer spirea *(Spiraea* x *bumalda* Anthony Waterer) is a dense, compact plant with an

Vanhoutte spirea is the last and one of the most profusely blooming spring-flowering spireas. It is a shrub that needs room for show.

A close view of Anthony Waterer spirea shows that all of the magenta flowers do not open at once and that an occasional branch will be marked with white variegation.

irregular, spreading habit. It sports profuse, flat-topped clusters of deep magenta flowers in early summer that continue sporadically through August. The flat green foliage with occasional white variegation is sure identification of this plant. The shrub's manageable size (about 3 feet tall) makes it a favorite.

Gold Flame (*Spiraea* x *bumalda* Gold Flame) is named for its unusually light-colored, yellow to yellow-green foliage. In spring, showy new growth is mottled with red, copper, and orange; these colors return in the fall. The pinkish flowers appear all summer.

Alpine (*Spiraea japonica* Alpina) is a low, spreading dwarf that grows little more than 2½ feet tall and 4 to 5 feet wide. It blooms in midsummer, showing many clusters of rose-crimson flowers.

Little Princess® (*Spiraea* x *bumalda* Little Princess) is slightly more upright and not as spreading as Alpine spirea. It has light green foliage and deep rose flowers that are delicately displayed in midsummer.

Limemound® (*Spiraea* x *bumalda* Limemound) is a low form with bright lime green foliage and soft violet flowers. The new spring growth is light red, which attracts as much attention as the flowers.

Alpine spirea is a tidy little plant that works well in mixed borders.

The leaves of Gold Flame spirea are a bright contrast to other perennials and shrubs.

AT A GLANCE
❖
SUMMER-FLOWERING SPIREAS
Spiraea species and hybrids

Features: profuse rose-colored flowers, delicate form

Foliage: deciduous

Height: 3 feet

Width: 4 or 5 feet

Light: full sun

Soil: rich, well drained

Water: moderate

Range: Zones 3 to 9

Pests: none specific

Remarks: a fresh addition of flowers for the summer garden

Viburnum

In late summer, doublefile viburnum is covered with clusters of red berries.

To select one viburnum from the dozens available is a delightful dilemma. They vary widely in form, flowers, and appearance. They may be deciduous or evergreen and are bothered by very few pests.

Regardless of where you plant viburnum, the plant's spectacular flowers, colorful fruit, steady form, and foliage color bring it to the forefront. The variety in viburnums means that you can pick a certain plant to fill a specific garden need.

Doublefile Viburnum

Doublefile viburnum grows rapidly to 15 feet tall and 18 feet wide. Because of the multitrunked form and horizontal branching, this shrub has the landscape effect of a small tree. The deep green foliage layers on top of the branches, emphasizing their horizontal structure. The dark green leaves are deeply veined for a rough-textured, leathery look.

The flowers of doublefile viburnum are borne in two parallel rows along each branch in a very unusual and eye-catching layered display. In the center of the bloom is a group of tiny yellow flowers that later will form seeds. Surrounding them is a ring of large white flowers similar to those of a lacecap French hydrangea.

In summer, doublefile viburnum bears fleshy fruit that is enclosed in a hard covering. This fruit turns bright red and then gradually turns black if it is not eaten by birds. In fall, the foliage turns a vivid scarlet, giving doublefile viburnum a final show before the leaves drop for winter.

AT A GLANCE
❖
DOUBLEFILE VIBURNUM
Viburnum plicatum var. *tomentosum*

Features: distinctive horizontal branches, white flowers, abundant fruit

Foliage: deciduous

Height: 5 to 15 feet

Width: 10 to 18 feet

Light: full sun to partial shade

Soil: moist, well drained

Water: moderate

Range: Zones 5 to 8

Pests: none specific

Remarks: may be used as a small tree

Doublefile viburnum wears its flowers in rows atop its horizontal branches.

114

In the Landscape

Doublefile viburnum may be used as an accent in a large, open lawn where its lower branches will reach to the ground. It can be trained as a small tree with room to pass beneath it. Placed at the corner of a foundation planting, it softens the vertical line of the house. The markedly horizontal branching pattern makes an excellent contrast to fences with vertical boards.

Planting and Care

Doublefile viburnum has a shallow, fibrous root system and it needs moist, rich, well-drained soil. It does not like heavy, poorly drained clay but will grow in either acid or slightly alkaline soil. The plant is hardy in Zones 5 to 8. South of Zone 7, partial shade is best, especially in the afternoon. Avoid reflected heat from buildings or pavement.

Different Selections

Mariesii has large flowers that are slightly raised above the branches to put even greater emphasis on the horizontal branching. Pink Beauty has pink petals. Shasta is a smaller plant (6 feet tall and 12 feet wide) with large, 4- to 6-inch flowers.

Linden Viburnum

Although demure through spring and summer, in fall Linden viburnum lights up with a cherry red blaze of fruit and red to purple leaves that make it worthy of a prominent spot in a garden. It is a broad, upright plant, growing 10 to 12 feet tall and 8 to 10 feet wide. In early spring, lustrous dark green leaves emerge before the creamy white flowers. The showy blooms last only a week. By late summer, the flowers mature into brilliant red fruits that adorn the branches until withered by a freeze.

In the Landscape

Linden viburnum is most effective when planted in a natural setting, such as the edge of a woodland area. It blends well with native plants, such as rhododendron and oakleaf hydrangea. You may also use it as an informal deciduous shrub. The berries and the dense foliage make linden viburnum an excellent shelter and food source for birds.

Linden viburnum's glossy fruit persists after the foliage turns bright red and then drops.

AT A GLANCE
❖
LINDEN VIBURNUM
Viburnum dilatatum

Features: splendid red fruit, upright form

Foliage: deciduous

Height: 3 to 12 feet

Width: 5 to 12 feet

Light: full sun to partial shade

Soil: moist, well drained

Water: moderate

Range: Zones 5 to 7

Pests: none specific

Remarks: grown primarily for its outstanding show of berries in late summer and fall

Catskill, a dwarf selection of linden viburnum, bears clusters of creamy white flowers that precede the berries in spring.

Planting and Care

Plant linden viburnum in full sun from Zone 7 northward and in partial shade in Zone 7. It prefers moist, well-drained, slightly acid soil but will also tolerate slightly alkaline soil.

Different Selections

Iroquois is a dense, rounded selection that grows 9 to 12 feet tall and equally wide, bearing an exceptional crop of fruits. Erie is more compact, growing to 6 to 8 feet tall and just as wide, with red translucent fruit that turns coral after a freeze. Catskill is a slow-growing dwarf (3 to 5 feet tall) for small gardens or courtyards.

Linden viburnum looks at home at the edge of the garden where it brings a dressy red berry show to the woodland setting.

European Cranberrybush Viburnum

The common name distinguishes European cranberrybush viburnum *(Viburnum opulus)* from a native viburnum, American cranberry viburnum *(Viburnum trilobum)* that is very similar but not as frequently available.

European cranberrybush viburnum grows at a moderate rate to 8 to 10 feet tall and 10 to 15 feet wide. The plant is an upright, multistemmed shrub with arching branches that reach to the ground, creating a rounded form. The foliage resembles a maple leaf but is smaller. After the foliage emerges in spring, the white flowers appear in broad, flat-topped, 2- to 3-inch-wide clusters. In late summer and early fall, the shrub bears cranberry-sized bright red fruit that is vivid against the dark, coarse-looking foliage; the fruit remains through winter in a spectacular show.

In fall, the foliage may turn yellow red and then reddish purple, but do not count on a spectacular show; sometimes the green leaves will simply fade and then fall from the plant.

In the Landscape

This is a viburnum for seasonal effect. It has a rugged look and naturalizes well, bringing brilliant fruit in fall and winter. It works well in drifts at the edge of a woodland, especially in front of contrasting evergreen trees, such as Norway spruce or white pine.

Planting and Care

European cranberrybush viburnum prefers full sun and will grow in wet or well-drained soil. In Zone 7, it needs afternoon shade. This shrub is very cold hardy and does not like hot weather.

Different Selections

Compacta is prized for its smaller size (only 5 or 6 feet tall and wide) and profuse flowers and fruit. Roseum, the common "European snowball" of older gardens, has larger, more showy, sterile flowers that are about 3 inches in diameter. The new growth and flower buds of Roseum seem to attract aphids more than other viburnums, which are generally pest free.

Snowball viburnum is named for its round clusters of blooms.

AT A GLANCE
❖
EUROPEAN CRANBERRYBUSH VIBURNUM
Viburnum opulus

Features: splendid white flowers, ornamental red fruit
Foliage: deciduous
Height: 5 to 10 feet
Width: 6 to 12 feet
Light: full sun to partial shade
Soil: moist, well drained
Water: moderate
Range: Zones 3 to 7
Pests: none specific
Remarks: bright berries in the fall garden

David viburnum is valued for its leathery leaves and fragrant blooms.

Other Viburnums

There are many other excellent viburnums. Evergreen viburnums are landscape staples in the lower and coastal South. The fragrant viburnums have perfumes as enchanting as gardenia. All prefer a moist, well-drained soil. They will decline in poorly drained locations.

David viburnum *(Viburnum davidii)* has lovely blue-green, leathery evergreen foliage and grows into a low, layered mound rarely more than 4 feet high. The flowers are white and are borne in dense, 3-inch-wide clusters. Not tolerant of extreme heat or cold, David viburnum should be planted in an area where it is sheltered from extreme winter winds, reflected heat, and afternoon sun. It is hardy from Zones 7 to 9 but never gets quite as lush in the South as it does in the Pacific Northwest, where the climate is more moderate. Because of its small size and handsome foliage, you may use it as a specimen or mix it with other shrubs in a border.

Koreanspice viburnum *(Viburnum carlesii)* grows into a rounded, dense form with stiff, upright branches, reaching 4 to 5 feet tall and equally wide. It will tolerate full sun but appreciates afternoon shade in the South. Koreanspice viburnum grows well from Zones 4 to 8, producing 3-inch-wide, globe-shaped clusters of spicy-sweet flowers. Use Koreanspice viburnum in a shrub border or at the edge of woods where you can enjoy its fragrance and let it fade into the background when not in bloom and in winter when it is leafless.

Sandankwa viburnum *(Viburnum suspensum)* generally reaches about 8 feet in both height and width, forming a rounded, evergreen mass that is a landscaping staple in Zones 9 and 10. The foliage is rounded and slightly toothed. Fragrant, pinkish-white flowers emerge in early summer, followed by bright red fruit. Because of its dense foliage and fast growth, this shrub is often used for screening.

Laurustinus viburnum *(Viburnum tinus)* is an indispensable upright, rounded evergreen shrub for the lower and coastal South. Hardy in Zones 7 to 10, the plant will reach 8 to 12 feet tall and 6 to 8 feet wide. The foliage is dense and medium textured; the flowers are pink to white. The plant is upright and rounded in form and grows well in either full sun or shade and, in fact, is well suited to use in poor soils. There is also a lower growing form that is popular for foundation planting.

Judd viburnum *(Viburnum x juddii)* is one of the best fragrant viburnums. A broad, spreading plant, it grows steadily to 15 feet tall and about 10 feet wide. In midspring it produces a ball-like

Koreanspice viburnum's blooms have a strong, exotic fragrance.

cluster of flowers about 3 inches wide after the leaves unfurl. This shrub has handsome deciduous foliage and black fruits in late summer. Use it at the corner of a foundation planting, to greet guests with fragrance along a long driveway, or as part of a shrub border.

Sweet viburnum *(Viburnum odoratissimum)* is easy to identify by its bright 4- to 6-inch-long evergreen leaves that give the shrub a coarse texture. It grows rapidly to an upright form, reaching 10 to 15 feet in height. It is often used as a screen or it may be grown as a small tree. In spring, sweet viburnum bears fragrant white flowers. Sometimes it produces a few red fruits that turn black as they mature. It will grow in Zones 8 to 10, although the tops may be killed back by severe freezes in Zone 8.

Wax Myrtle

Wax myrtle is popular as an evergreen screen.

Wax myrtle combines utility and grace for use in any style garden. In addition to its design flexibility, wax myrtle also adapts to different growing conditions—full sun, partial shade, dry or soggy soil, or even beachside.

Native from Maryland to Texas and Florida, wax myrtle grows rapidly into a wide, rounded evergreen at least 10 to 15 feet high and equally wide. In the lower and coastal South, it will reach treelike proportions (15 to 20 feet in height and spread), casting a mottled shade similar to that of willow oak. Its hallmark is narrow leaves that have a bayberry scent when crushed and give the plant a wispy appearance.

Female plants have inconspicuous flowers in early spring that will develop small gray berries if a male plant is nearby.

In the Landscape

The soft, delicate texture of wax myrtle blends nicely with coarse, broad-leafed evergreens, such as cleyera and pittosporum. The evergreen foliage also provides a good background for such deciduous plants as oakleaf hydrangea and forsythia.

One of wax myrtle's most common uses is as a screen or hedge along the property line. The fine foliage and multibranched, twiggy habit make it easy to shear into an architectural hedge. Wax myrtle is also a natural complement to young pines for screening both high and low views.

At the beach, wax myrtle blocks salt spray to create a shelter for less salt-tolerant plants. Because it can withstand temperature extremes, wax myrtle is one of the better shrubs for parking lots. The same quality also makes it an excellent evergreen for a large container on a deck or a patio.

AT A GLANCE
❖
WAX MYRTLE
Myrica cerifera

Features: graceful foliage, rapid growth

Foliage: evergreen

Height: 10 to 20 feet

Width: 15 to 20 feet

Light: full sun to partial shade

Soil: any type

Water: low

Range: Zones 7 to 9

Pests: none specific

Remarks: one of the most versatile large evergreen shrubs

Wax myrtle is vigorous and grows rapidly, especially in the lower and coastal South. Should it outgrow its location, reduce its height or width by removing the offending branches entirely. Or prune the lower branches away and turn it into a treelike shrub, revealing the silver-gray trunk.

Planting and Care

Wax myrtle tolerates a wide variety of soil types, even clay, but grows best in the sandy, well-drained soil typical of the coastal plain. However, it will adapt to soggy sites; in the wild it grows everywhere from sand dunes to swamps. It will thrive in sun or partial shade, but the shadier the location, the more sparse the foliage.

In the lower and coastal South and the warmer sections of the middle South, wax myrtle is durably evergreen. The foliage may burn if the temperature plunges to zero. In the middle South, ice poses the greatest risk, with the fairly lightweight branches breaking under the weight. However, well-established plants will rejuvenate quickly from the base.

Wax myrtle is one of the best large shrubs for any garden. Here it is used as a small tree.

Different Selections

Except for a finely textured dwarf form, wax myrtle is sold primarily as a species with few named selections. However, seedlings and clones grown from cuttings tend to be locally adapted. For example, a wax myrtle native to south Georgia may not be reliably evergreen in North Carolina, so check with your garden center for one that was locally grown.

Weigela

Weigela's springtime flowers burst into bloom from the previous year's growth after the leaves have emerged.

From the shrub borders of generations past comes the sprawling, worry-free weigela with its mid-spring show of multicolored trumpet-shaped flowers. Growing quickly to between 6 and 9 feet tall and 9 to 12 feet wide, weigela loosely resembles forsythia in form and growth habit. Unlike forsythia, however, it blooms after the leaves have emerged. The flowers may be white, red, pink, or maroon.

Weigela is joyous in bloom (some selections are also fragrant) but unremarkable after the flowers have faded. There is little fall color and the fruit has minimal ornamental value; winter finds a tangled, twiggy thicket. However, the redeeming quality, in addition to the splendid, varied colors of different selections, is the plant's vigor. It grows profusely under poor conditions and with little care. Its tolerance for pollution makes it a truly industrial-strength flowering shrub and one that will give a one-season show that is worth the three-season wait.

In the Landscape

Weigela looks best in a shrub border, placed where the profusion of flowers will be visible during spring but the shrub may recede during the remainder of the year. You may also plant weigela as an informal hedge or deciduous barrier, but it is best used in conjunction with architecture or fencing. Here again the use parallels that of forsythia, with the important admonition that weigela, while wonderful in flower, is not a dressy shrub. There is a loosely bunched quality about weigela when out of bloom that makes it better suited to a rustic setting than a formal scheme.

Planting and Care

Weigela needs full sun for the most profuse flowering but will benefit from light, afternoon shade in the deep South. It also prefers fertile, well-drained soil but is extremely adaptable and will grow in poor soil that drains well.

AT A GLANCE
❖

WEIGELA
Weigela florida

Features: spreading form; profuse, trumpet-shaped flowers

Foliage: deciduous

Height: 3 to 9 feet

Width: 4 to 12 feet

Light: full sun to partial shade

Soil: well drained

Water: moderate

Range: Zones 4 to 9

Pests: none specific

Remarks: widely adaptable, rugged shrub known for its one-season show

You can keep weigela blooming year after year by pruning it as it ages. Prune established plants just after they bloom; use loppers to thin the plant, removing the oldest canes close to the base. This will encourage vigorous growth that will produce prolific bloom and slightly limits the shrub's size. It is normal for some of the stems to die back each year. Simply remove them by cutting them at the base.

Different Selections

Abel Carriere is a proven selection with large scarlet flowers that have gold throats. Candida is an old favorite with pure white flowers. Conquerant is another old plant with very large, deep pink flowers. Eva Rathke is a slow-growing selection with a compact habit; the blooming continues a bit longer than most. Mont Blanc is an old, very popular weigela because of its vigor and fragrant white flowers. Pink Princess is known for its cold hardiness (it was developed in Iowa) and has lavender-pink blossoms. Variegata has deep rose flowers and white-edged leaves. Variegata Nana has the same foliage as Variegata but only grows to about 3 feet tall.

Weigela's flower-laden branches mound upon themselves.

Flower colors of weigela include deep pink, red, white, and maroon.

Pests and Diseases

The following insects and diseases are common pests of the shrubs in this book. Timing is very important when controlling these insects, as you must kill the first generation before they are able to reproduce and cause more damage. Insects and diseases are most damaging to a shrub that is already weakened by poor growing conditions or other reasons, so remember that the best form of control is to maintain the overall health of the shrub.

Many techniques and pesticides are available to help you fight insect pests, but the recommendations for using these products change frequently. Try mild pesticides, such as insecticidal soap, before using stronger substances. Always use pesticides strictly according to label directions. For information about specific pesticides, please contact your local Extension office, which is listed under the county Department of Agriculture in your blue pages.

Aphids

Aphids are tiny, pear-shaped insects that are about ⅛ to ¼ inch long; they are frequently green or black but may also be yellow or pink. They harm shrubs by sucking sap from the tender young leaves, stems, and buds so that growth is distorted and the buds do not open.

Aphids are usually worst in spring and fall. They will produce hundreds of offspring in a few weeks, so it is crucial to control them as soon as they appear. These pests may disappear on their own once the temperature reaches 90 degrees.

Beetles

Beetles are hard-bodied insects that chew on the leaves and tender stems of shrubs. While most fly in and out of shrubs and trees, feeding without noticeable damage, they occasionally reach outlandish numbers and can strip a shrub of its leaves.

Beetles are very difficult to control once they begin to cause a problem. They usually feed in hordes, with hundreds present at one time. Dusting foliage with a recommended pesticide helps, but you must keep the dust on new growth as it unfurls. The best way to control beetles is to kill the larvae, called **grubs,** which feed on lawn grasses. To do this most effectively, join forces with your neighbors, who are doubtless being affected by this pest as well, to treat a large area.

Caterpillars

Caterpillars are the larvae of moths and butterflies. They generally feed on a plant's leaves without your knowledge and without causing any serious damage. A few caterpillars, such as the young gypsy moth, can be devastating. If you see serious damage due to the feeding of caterpillars, your shrubs need the care of a professional.

Fire Blight

Fire blight is a bacterial disease that causes a shrub's leaves, flowers, and branches to suddenly turn black and die, as if they have been burned. You can control fire blight by spraying early in the spring while the shrubs are in bloom, as the bacteria is often spread by bees visiting the flowers.

Lacebugs

Lacebugs feed on the leaves, sucking sap and causing the leaves to dry, curl, and fall from the shrub. A tell-tale sign of this feeding is tiny black spots on the underside of the leaves. These insects have lacy wings and are flat and oval or rectangular in outline. The nymphs are elongated, wingless, and spiny. Lacebugs frequently damage andromeda, azalea, and cotoneaster.

Shrubs attacked by lacebugs in spring or early summer need treatment to prevent defoliation. In late summer, treatment is not as critical because the plant has already manufactured food for winter storage.

Leaf Miners

Leaf miners are tiny larvae that tunnel and feed between the upper and lower surfaces of a leaf, leaving blisters and serpentine trails or "mines" that disfigure the leaf; azaleas are their frequent target. Leaf miners are generally the young of flies, beetles, sawflies, or moths and will appear as small, oblong larvae at the fresh end of a mine. Many shrubs can tolerate feeding by leaf miners without serious damage. However, if the miners are eating more than one-third of the leaf's surface, it is best to control them, as they are reducing the amount of food-manufacturing cells in the leaf. To control the infestation, spray the shrub with a systemic pesticide.

Root Knot Nematodes

Root knot nematodes are not insects but rather microscopic, eel-like pests that attack the roots of a plant. Plants infected with nematodes may stop growing or begin to yellow and die back if root damage is extensive. There is little you can do to get rid of root knot nematodes if your soil is infested. However, they do not seem to be as damaging if the soil is rich; when planting, add plenty of compost or other organic matter to avert this pest. It also helps to keep the plants in optimum condition with plenty of water and fertilizer so that they are better able to compensate for the root damage. Boxwoods are especially susceptible, particularly those growing in sandy soils. However, Japanese boxwood seems to be immune to these pests.

Scales

Scales may be soft- or hard-bodied insects that cling to the underside of leaves and along stems, sucking the sap from the shrub. The hard-bodied types look like tiny raised surfaces on the leaf or stem and can be scraped away with a fingernail. Soft-bodied types do not have this covering but may be covered in white wax or a mass of cottonlike fibers. Scales often attack camellias.

It is important to control scales when they first appear and while they are looking for a place to feed; they are harder to kill as they get older. The eggs are naturally resistant to pesticides, so you must spray more than once to kill young scales as they emerge. In winter, spray the shrub's branches with dormant oil to smother the eggs, preventing them from hatching in spring.

Spider Mites

Spider mites are tiny, spiderlike pests that collect on the underside of leaves and on flower buds. They damage shrubs by sucking sap, leaving the leaves deformed and the buds unopened. They are worst in spring and fall, especially during dry weather. You may not see spider mites until their feeding begins to make the tops of the leaves look faded and mottled. Turning a leaf over will reveal clusters of pinpoint-sized spider mites and often their delicate webbing; use a magnifying glass to be sure. Boxwood, cotoneaster, and Chinese holly are among their favorite shrubs.

It is important to control a serious infestation, as spider mites multiply quickly. They can reduce the ability of a tree to manufacture food, especially if they appear in spring. To control spider mites, you must thoroughly coat the underside of the leaves with pesticide. They may disappear on their own when the temperature climbs to 90 degrees or higher.

Index

Index

Special Thanks

Monrovia Nursery Company, photographs, 60, 72, 118, 119

Southern Progress Corporation Library Staff

Christina Wynn